"*Never Enough* is a rich th. a theological ivory tower. It was written from Sarah Ivill's heart as a life message grounded in biblical truth. Her transparency and practical insights invite women, young and not-so-young, to dismantle the world's deceptive definition of beauty and achievement with the power of the gospel. The author leads us straight to Jesus to embrace His truth that sets us free. As women learn to replace error with truth, the chains of spiritual bondage are crushed and Christ alone defines our worth, beauty, and significance—*setting us free indeed!*"

—Leslie Bennett, women's ministry initiatives and leader connection blog manager, Revive Our Hearts

"After discipling and counseling countless women who have struggled with eating disorders on the college campus over the past five years, I find that this is one of the most effective books at addressing the overwhelmingly common struggle of body image for women in today's culture. Not only does Sarah Ivill speak to the issue directly but she even does the hard work of digging down to the motives of our hearts as women. This is certainly an amazing resource for women of all ages today!"

—Joni Clayton, director of development, Campus Outreach Charlotte

"In *Never Enough* Sarah Ivill shows the reader that Christ is always more than enough. With beautiful vulnerability and rich theological insight, Ivill invites her readers into her own struggles with shame, comparison, and the search for her true worth. She explains how the truth that set her free is an offer to all as she points us over and over again to the hope of the gospel and the power of Christ. I highly recommend this study!"

—Courtney Doctor, coordinator of women's training and content, The Gospel Coalition; speaker, Bible teacher, and author of *From Garden to Glory: A Bible Study on the Bible's Story*

"God faithfully challenges and encourages me when I read Sarah Ivill's writing. He challenges me through her scriptural depth and the beautiful way she applies God's truth to the 'real stuff' of life, like body envy, ministry discontentment, or success comparison. And God encourages me through Sarah's ability to unpack His trustworthy promises of love, sovereignty, and provision into the areas of life in which we each need consistent reorientation to 'bounce our eyes' back to Jesus Christ. *Never Enough* is a wonderful gem for all who struggle to believe that they are precious in God's sight."

—Ellen Mary Dykas, women's ministry coordinator, Harvest USA

"Sarah's vulnerability draws us into the journey of her painful trial. She invites us to join her in finding hope, healing, and comfort as she takes us from the sting of shame to Jesus singing over her in triumph. 'Blessed be the God and Father of our Lord Jesus Christ, the Father of mercies and God of all comfort, who comforts us in all our tribulation, that we may be able to comfort those who are in any trouble, with the comfort with which we ourselves are comforted by God' (2 Cor. 1:3–4)."

—Bernie and Pat Lawrence, senior associate pastor and wife, Christ Covenant Church

"*Never Enough* contains wonderful biblical wisdom in a voice we would love for our daughters and granddaughters to hear. Sarah clearly and compassionately understands the body-image and approval struggles women go through (especially when they are younger) and points them to how they can find their significance, beauty, and perfection in Christ. We love how she weaves in the stories of women in the Bible and her own story as she addresses these issues so effectively. Our favorite summary is 'Christ frees us from the slavery to girl power so that we can be servants filled with His power.'"

—Jim and Caroline Newheiser, biblical counselors, Reformed Theological Seminary, Charlotte *never enough*

never enough

Confronting Lies about Appearance and Achievement with Gospel Hope

Sarah Ivill

Reformation Heritage Books
Grand Rapids, Michigan

Never Enough
© 2019 by Sarah Ivill

Reformation Heritage Books
2965 Leonard St. NE
Grand Rapids, MI 49525
616-977-0889
orders@heritagebooks.org
www.heritagebooks.org

Printed in the United States of America
19 20 21 22 23 24/10 9 8 7 6 5 4 3 2 1

Library of Congress Cataloging-in-Publication Data

Names: Ivill, Sarah, author.
Title: Never enough : confronting lies about appearance and achievement with
    Gospel hope / Sarah Ivill.
Description: Grand Rapids, Michigan : Reformation Heritage Books, 2019. |
    Includes bibliographical references.
Identifiers: LCCN 2019020145 (print) | LCCN 2019022287 (ebook) | ISBN
    9781601786777 (epub) | ISBN 9781601786760 (pbk. : alk. paper)
Subjects: LCSH: Christian women—Religious life. | Body image in women—
    Religious aspects—Christianity.
Classification: LCC BV4527 (ebook) | LCC BV4527 .I95 2019 (print) | DDC
    306.4/613—dc23
LC record available at https://lccn.loc.gov/2019020145

For additional Reformed literature, request a free book list from Reformation Heritage Books at the above regular or email address.

To the One who answered me out of my distress,
Who brought my life up from the pit.
Salvation is of the Lord!

And to my sisters who find their
lives fainting away
As they pay regard to vain idols,
May you know His salvation! (Jonah 2:1, 6–9)

September 2021

Contents

Foreword

The day I learned my daughter had an eating disorder, we were in the car together for the first time since she had gotten her driver's license the month before. I had missed this time with her; traditionally it had always been where our best conversations took place. That day was no different. Yet it was totally different from what I ever expected.

Before I even backed out of the driveway, she blurted out the secret she had been carrying and was no longer able to bear the weight of alone: "Mom, I've been making myself throw up."

Most of what followed is a blur to me now. I remember wanting to pull the car over so I could hold her tight and fighting back tears as I listened to my precious girl share about the worthlessness she felt. How was it even possible for her to think she was *never enough*?

Of course, as her mom I'm partial. But when I tell you *gorgeous*, *popular*, *talented*, *funny*, *compassionate*, and *well liked* were the words often used to describe her, I am not exaggerating. She was the type of girl others might look at and think she had it all together. Perfect, even.

But for my daughter nothing could be further from the truth. Unknown to me, she was constantly evaluating how she thought she stacked up to others. Whether she was walking the halls at school or scrolling through social media, these comparisons were endless. In her mind everyone was skinnier, prettier, smarter, wealthier, more talented, or a better athlete. And it all translated into her feeling as if she were not enough, that she was less-than and worthless.

I know my daughter is far from alone in such struggles with identity and worth. I also know the striving to attain and maintain a certain standard isn't limited to those in their teens. In this book Sarah Ivill highlights her own story as well as the stories of women even in the Bible who, as she explains, "battled the temptation to covet and compare." So if you have picked up this book feeling all alone, be assured you are not.

The "comparison cage," as Sarah appropriately calls it, stems all the way back to the garden when Adam and Eve bought into the serpent's lies that life was found somewhere other than in God. And just like they saw and took the fruit thinking it would give them something more, we too "exchange the truth of God for the lie, and [worship] and [serve] the creature rather than the Creator" (Rom. 1:25).

We look to our own wisdom, to our appearance, performance, relationships, and success to fill our longing for love, acceptance, significance, and worth. But the harder we try to secure an identity in things that can't fill us, the emptier and more desperate we become. For my daughter, this is what led to her eating disorder.

But my daughter and Sarah's greatest problem (as Sarah will share with you) was not with food. Their greatest problem—as with all of us—is a heart problem. Or as Sarah puts it, "a worship disorder," not an eating disorder.

And that's just it. It is why Sarah has written this book: to expose the false identities we turn to as we look for identity and worth—in other words, the lies we believe about ourselves and how they spiral us down. But Sarah doesn't stop with the diagnosis; she leads us to the source of true help and healing in Christ Jesus, whose love, acceptance, *and* identity we have secured. Knowing who He is for us is the truth we need to replace the lies.

We get tripped up, though, because remembering who we are in Christ is not a one-and-done thing. It is a battle. This is not what we who want a quick fix like to hear. Certainly as a mother I wanted nothing more than to quickly and permanently wipe away my daughter's struggles. But in this, God revealed my own false god of control, leading me to see my struggle with not accepting circumstances that were outside of my command. Ultimately, just as my daughter was not resting in Christ's work and worth for her, neither was I. I was trying to be my own savior—and hers. But if Christ's acceptance of us is based on His perfect record (and it is), then we are free from having to be perfect, or even having to be okay! And so the message of this book is what I needed to hear again too.

I hope that as you read *Never Enough* what you discover, or rediscover, is that because Jesus was enough and His record is yours, you are enough. May this bring to you great freedom and rest and, by His grace, the perseverance to fix your eyes on Christ in a world that values what is fading away.

> —Kristen Hatton, author of *The Gospel-Centered Life in Exodus*, *Face Time: Your Identity in a Selfie World*, and *Get Your Story Straight*

A Note from Sarah

This book is a result of the response I received from sharing my testimony in fall 2017 with a women's Bible study that was composed mostly of young professionals, as well as from subsequent emails over the next few months asking me for prayer or help regarding a loved one battling an eating disorder. After one of my pastor's wives encouraged me that my testimony was something that needed to be heard in middle schools, high schools, and college campuses, as well as women's Bible studies, my heart was set with the theme for my next book. By God's grace the Lord moved the project forward by opening the door with my publisher, for which I am exceedingly grateful.

At the same time, I was becoming increasingly aware through articles, pediatricians, pastors, and friends that social media, particularly Instagram, was extremely harmful for young women. In fact, it was becoming a life-or-death matter for some young women who turned to eating disorders because they weren't getting enough likes or comments on their social media posts. If eating disorders were rampant during my high school days—and they were—how much more are they today among girls receiving a steady stream of images on social media with which to compare or compete? Recent research confirms these claims. In one study regarding body image and performance, teens were asked why they felt inferior (or less-than): 59 percent said because of appearance (body image), 49 percent because of ability (performance), 38 percent because of intelligence (performance), and 35 percent because of size (body image).[1]

In another study teens were asked why they were so anxious about what was happening online and why they were so fascinated with social media. Their responses included the following: 61 percent were checking to see if their posts were getting likes and comments; 36 percent were checking to see if their peers were doing things without them; and 21 percent said they were checking to make sure nothing unkind was being said about them.[2] It is not just teens who are tempted to compare or compete with what they see on social media or in the lives of those around them. Women of all ages continue to battle body image and performance lies. In preparing the manuscript for this book, I asked female readers as young as their early teens and as old as their seventies to provide feedback. All of them found applicable material for their lives in these pages.

---

1. Kristen Hatton, "Behind the Screens of the Selfie World of Teens," *By Faith: The Online Magazine of the Presbyterian Church in America*, January 31, 2018, http://byfaithonline.com/behind-the-screens-of-the-selfie-world-of-teens/.

2. Hatton, "Behind the Screens of the Selfie World of Teens."

Throughout the chapters of this book, you will see how closely body image and performance were related in my own battle with lies that ultimately led to my addiction to thinness and fitness during my teenage years and early twenties. Perhaps that is why I want to write to the younger generation. My heart is tender toward them. I can relate to their battle, and I want to humbly help. But I don't just want to help the younger generation; I also want to help their mothers and grandmothers understand the lies behind the relentless pursuit of a pretty appearance and perfect achievements.

In one sense this book was one of the easiest for me to write. It is my story. But in another sense the fact that it is my story also made it one of the hardest. I am not proud of the lies my flesh has been so prone to believe. And I'm not proud of the actions I've taken because of it. But God's Word says, "Blessed be the God and Father of our Lord Jesus Christ, the Father of mercies and God of all comfort, who comforts us in all our tribulation, that we may be able to comfort those who are in any trouble, with the comfort with which we ourselves are comforted by God" (2 Cor. 1:3–4). And so I have tried to be transparent in these pages, offering you the comfort that I received from our heavenly Father and our Lord and Savior Jesus Christ and His Spirit, who helps us in our weakness and enables us to say no to the flesh and yes to the things of God. Although I am no longer addicted to thinness and fitness, I don't want to leave you with the impression that I've triumphed over the five lies I will be discussing in this book. Each day I am tempted to believe at least one, if not several, of them. I have to diligently pray that the Lord will strengthen me against them. And when I fall, I always find the forgiving arms of my heavenly Father opened wide to me.

In the introduction I give you the testimony I recounted to the women's Bible study group composed mostly of young professionals. I don't return to my addiction to thinness and fitness until chapter 6. In between I expose five lies that laid the foundation for my addiction, which began in high school, lasted through college, and ended in seminary. In chapter 1 I address the lie that our ways are better than God's ways and our wisdom is better than His wisdom. Chapter 2 considers the lie that we have to look like "her" (whether it's a supermodel, one of our peers, or one of our sisters in Christ) in order to be beautiful. In chapter 3 I deal with the lie that our beauty and significance are defined by whether or not a man loves us. I explore the lie that our significance is based on our success as defined by our superiors in chapter 4. And in chapter 5 I conclude with the lie that if we had what "she" has then we would be more satisfied, significant, and successful than we are now.

In chapter 6, after sharing how these lies led to the perfect storm in my own life and recounting my battle with an addiction to thinness and fitness, I conclude the book with the grand hope that the truth of God's Word sets us free from "the sin which so easily ensnares us" so that we can "run with endurance the race that is set before us, looking unto Jesus, the author and finisher of our faith, who for the joy that was set before Him endured the cross, despising the shame, and has sat down at the right hand of the throne of God" (Heb. 12:1–2). It is to this throne that we are invited to run when the idols of this world seemingly overtake us: "For we do not have a High Priest who cannot sympathize with our weaknesses, but was in all points tempted as we are, yet without sin. Let us therefore come boldly to the throne of grace, that we may obtain mercy and find grace to help in time of need" (Heb. 4:15–16).

It is my sincere desire that you will read this book and answer the questions at the close of each chapter within the context of the local church. This was vital for me in my own battle with these lies. Lies are much easier to believe in isolation than they are in community. It would be wonderful for an older group of women to study this with a younger group of women, or for mothers and daughters to read this book together, or for a women's Bible study composed of women from various stages of life to study these chapters together. As you do so, I hope and pray you are convicted in your sin, comforted in your shame, challenged in your beliefs, and changed by the truth of God's Word.

My prayer is that "the God of peace who brought up our Lord Jesus from the dead, that great Shepherd of the sheep, through the blood of the everlasting covenant, [will] make you complete in every good work to do His will, working in you what is well pleasing in His sight, through Jesus Christ, to whom be glory forever and ever. Amen" (Heb. 13:20–21).

Acknowledgments

There are several people I need to thank for being part of this project. Melissa McPhail's invitation to share my testimony in front of a women's Bible study group, although I didn't know it at the time, was the launching point of this book. She went on to be a reader of the initial manuscript, giving encouraging feedback. Pat Lawrence, one of our pastor's wives in attendance when I shared my testimony, encouraged me to take this message to girls as young as middle school. She and her husband, Bernie Lawrence (senior associate pastor at Christ Covenant Church), read an early version of the manuscript, giving several practical suggestions. Andrea Johnson, Joni Clayton, and Kara and Gabrielle Girrard all read early versions of the book, providing insightful and encouraging feedback. I also want to thank the women's Bible study team at my church, which rallied around me in prayer support.

Thank you to my mom and dad, David and Judy Gelaude, who were my very first readers and who, in many ways, lived this story with me. Their love for me, patience with me, and support of me over the years has blessed me tremendously. My husband, Charles, also read the manuscript in detail, providing invaluable support and encouragement. My oldest children, Caleb and Hannah, provided constant encouragement and prayers. They, along with my younger children, Daniel and Lydia, are a constant reminder of my task to pass on the faith to the next generation. I want them to know their hope is not in their appearance or their achievements, but in the gospel of our Lord and Savior Jesus Christ. It is this gospel that the pastors of our church, Christ Covenant Church (PCA), faithfully proclaim Sunday after Sunday, for which I am deeply grateful.

Thank you to Reformation Heritage Books: Dr. Joel Beeke, for your personal encouragement to keep writing and your commitment to read each manuscript; and especially Jay Collier, for his support and valuable feedback; and Annette Gysen for once again having a keen editorial eye and encouraging tone.

Finally, thank you to my heavenly Father, to my Lord and Savior Jesus Christ, and to the Spirit, who helps me in my weakness. To the triune God be the glory for what He has done through me, a broken vessel and a flawed instrument, yet one that is in the grip of His mighty and gracious hand.

Introduction

It was my sophomore year of high school, and I was sitting around with my cross-country team listening to the older girls compare fat grams in bagel brands. If you have ever looked at bagel labels, you know that there is not any difference worth noting unless you are obsessed with your weight. Little did I know how influential that conversation, and many more like it, would become in my life. Add to that the billboards, magazines, and other media that boasted model-thin women all around me, and I bought into the lie "I have to look like 'her' in order to be beautiful." In other words, I believed that my worth was based on my outward appearance.

At the same time I was running cross-country, I was also playing basketball. Unlike the girls on my cross-country team, my teammates on my basketball team were not having conversations about fat grams in bagel brands. They could down a fast-food burger in no time at all and not think twice about it. And my coach certainly thought I could use a few burgers myself in order to put on some weight for my position as forward or center. There was another conversation going on though within basketball that was just as influential and just as damaging as the one on my cross-country team. It really wasn't a conversation at all. It was a coach with a temper who could fire off a cuss word, stomp his feet, clap his hands, and throw water, attempting to motivate us to play better and harder. Failing to live up to his expectations and thinking my significance was based on success as he defined it led me to believe another lie: "My worth is based on my outward performance." Failure to perform well led me to inflict punishment on myself, which matched perfectly with the motivation behind the other lie—if I didn't live up to my coach's expectations, then I didn't deserve to eat. As we have already seen, these twin themes of body image and performance are still at the heart of young women's search for beauty and worth today. But it is not just young women. Women of all ages struggle with defining their significance by their appearance and achievements.

By the time I was in college, my addiction to thinness and fitness was raging. *But God* intervened. I still remember sitting in my Hebrew class during my final exam with tears streaming down my face as I translated the verses in Jonah 2:5–6 from Hebrew to English:

> The waters surrounded me, even to my soul;
> The deep closed around me;
> Weeds were wrapped around my head.
> I went down to the moorings of the mountains;
> The earth with its bars closed behind me forever;
> *Yet You have brought up my life from the pit,*
> *O LORD, my God.* (italics mine)

Deliverance would not come overnight, but this was a turning point for me. If the Lord could radically deliver Jonah from the pit he was in, then He could also deliver me from what seemed like a prison. The hope that I had not found in a secular counselor's office, a support group for those battling addictions, or a nutritionist's office I found in the Word of God. It cut through the lies and gave me truth upon which to stand. This would prove critical over the next few years as I fought for freedom from my addiction.

By the time I reached seminary, I really wanted my addiction to thinness and fitness to be over. I had recognized my sin of trying to serve two masters. I realized that fitness and food had become idols in my life. I knew this because I *had* to exercise and eat healthy every day in order to feel good about myself. I wouldn't even go without exercise and healthy eating on a vacation because somewhere along the way I started relying on exercise and healthy eating for my hope and happiness, my significance and security.

I remember keeping a journal in which I would write down every lie that came across my mind and counter it with a scriptural truth. For example, if I thought I looked fat, I challenged whether or not that was really true (it wasn't), and then I moved on to passages that spoke of God looking at the heart instead of the outside of man (1 Sam. 16:7).

At some point, I also stopped weighing myself, recognizing that it could lead me down a pathway of destruction. And I started bouncing my eyes off billboards and magazines, recognizing those could also lead me down a pathway of deceit. So I was striving hard to put this addiction behind me. And since seminary days were filled with an immersion of studying Scripture, I was at a great place for healing.

But there was another dimension that was just as important as being immersed in truth, and that was being surrounded by the community of believers, some of whom I confided in regarding my addiction. This was helpful in numerous ways. First, I wasn't fighting alone. Individuals make terrible armies. But I had a group of sisters fighting with me. Their prayers, accountability, and encouragement meant a great deal to me. Second, when I confessed my sin to the Lord and to my sisters, it didn't seem to hold as much power over me. My sin was exposed. People knew. And in the publicity of it I began to see it for what it really was— lies I had believed. My worth isn't based on my outward appearance. It is based on the person and work of Jesus Christ. And my worth isn't based on my outward performance. It is based on the perfect performance of Christ on my behalf. It is the gospel that set me free—and continues to set me free when I'm once again tempted to believe the lies. The Lord ingrained deeply in me that Christ is enough for me. In a culture where we often compliment external beauty, even in the church, I needed someone to remind me that I'm not pretty apart from Christ, and no amount of makeovers or designer dresses will fix that. Apart from Christ, I am ugly and dead in my sins. I also needed someone to tell me that I will never perform perfectly and to seek perfection is futile. Christ alone is perfect. Knowing the truths that I didn't have to be thin and fit to be loved; that I didn't have to perform perfectly to be accepted; and that I am beautiful, loved, and accepted in Christ because Christ has performed perfectly and died for me was tremendously freeing.

Perhaps you are ensnared in an addiction today. The book of Proverbs tells us that addictions are like having a feast in a grave (see 9:13–18).[1] We think we are in the midst of a feast when we are actually in the midst of a famine. Through this book I want to invite you to exchange the lies for the truth and to rest in Jesus Christ. He is our hope and happiness, our security and significance.

---

1. Edward T. Welch has written a wonderful book that I highly recommend for people battling addictions: *Addictions—A Banquet in the Grave* (Phillipsburg, N.J.: P&R, 2001).

Chapter 1

Naked and Ashamed

My husband and I got engaged and married when I was twenty-four years old. For at least eleven years, I had struggled with body image. Several of my thoughts were recorded in prayer journals, excerpts of which I will share with you throughout this book. Five months before we got married, after reading Genesis 2:25, I wrote,

I am not feeling unashamed when I think about letting Charles look at my body [on our wedding night]. I begin to question whether he'll like it.... Oh, Father! Forgive me. I turn over to Psalm 139 and read that I am "fearfully and wonderfully made." You know me more intimately than Charles will ever know me, and you love me and accept me.... Charles is marrying me because he loves who I am—deep down inside.... Help me, Father, to get to the point by the night of our wedding where I can stand before him naked and not be ashamed.

Naked and Unashamed

On the sixth day of creation, the triune God created Adam
and Eve: "So God created man in His own image; in the
image of God He created him; male and female He created them" (Gen. 1:27). John Calvin says, "God's image
was visible in the light of the mind, in the uprightness of
the heart, and in the soundness of all the parts.… [It] is
the perfect excellence of human nature which shone in
Adam before his defection."[1] As the Westminster Shorter
Catechism, question 10, says, "God created man male and
female, after his own image, in knowledge, righteousness
and holiness, with dominion over the creatures."

After we read in Genesis 1:31, "God saw everything
that He had made, and indeed it was very good," it is sur-
prising to come to the verses in the next chapter that say,
"And the LORD God said, 'It is not good that man should be
alone; I will make him a helper comparable to him'" (2:18).
After Adam named all the animals, the narrative strikes a
somber chord: "But for Adam there was not found a helper
comparable to him" (v. 20). In another miraculous act of
creation, the Lord made woman from the rib of man and
then brought her to Adam. Adam's words resound with
hope fulfilled:

> This is now bone of my bones
> And flesh of my flesh;
> She shall be called Woman,
> Because she was taken out of Man (v. 23)

---

1. John Calvin, *Institutes of the Christian Religion*, ed. John T. McNeill,
trans. Ford Lewis Battles (Philadelphia: Westminster, 1960), 1.15.4.

The happy couple relishes the goodness of their Creator, their relationship, and the garden: "And they were both naked, the man and his wife, and were not ashamed" (v. 25).

As both naked and unashamed, they knew a life you and I have never known. It was a life of perfection. Contrarily, you and I have known the pain and futility of striving after perfection in a world that is no longer perfect.

Sin and Shame

Although Adam and Eve were perfect and didn't have to sin, they had not yet been confirmed in their perfected state, which meant they could sin. God gave them a test to see who would be king in their lives—God or the world, the devil, and their own flesh. Tragically, Adam and Eve chose the latter. Although Eve knew the kindness of the Lord and His commandments, she chose to sin by taking the fruit from the forbidden tree. Satan challenged God's kindness, kingship, and commandment when he suggested to Eve that God's word was not true, and Eve, in a moment of disordered desires, became a sinner and shared her disordered desires with her husband. Eve believed the lie: my ways are better than God's ways, and my wisdom is better than His wisdom.

Hideous sin led to the first hide-and-seek game in the history of mankind, but unlike the childhood game, which is filled with laughter and squealing, this game wasn't fun. The holy King had been disobeyed, and He was angry. No longer could Adam and Eve stand naked and unashamed. Instead, they were naked and ashamed. And not just Adam and Eve, but all their posterity who would come from them would be born in original sin.

How did this impact the image of God in us? Calvin says, "God's image was not totally annihilated and destroyed in him, yet it was so corrupted that whatever remains is frightful deformity.... [It] was subsequently so vitiated and almost blotted out that nothing remains after the ruin except what is confused, mutilated, and disease-ridden."[2]

Nakedness is not the problem. Sin is. God asks Adam and Eve, "Who told you that you were naked?" His follow-up question is instructive: "Have you eaten from the tree of which I commanded you that you should not eat?" (Gen. 3:11). Sin had revealed to them that they were naked. What follows is the first blame game in the history of the world. Adam blamed Eve, and then Eve blamed the serpent. God addresses them in exactly the opposite order—first the serpent (Satan), then Eve, and then Adam. The curse on the serpent affects his fortune ("cursed more than all cattle, and more than every beast of the field"), form ("on your belly you shall go"), food ("you shall eat dust"), and fight ("I will put enmity between you and the woman") (vv. 14–15). Eve faced sorrow with regard to her children and struggle with regard to her husband. Adam faced sweaty toil and the separation of body and soul at death. But by far the worst curse was the couple's exile from the garden and separation from the presence of God: "So He drove out the man; and He placed cherubim at the east of the garden

---

2. Calvin, *Institutes*, 1.15.4.

of Eden, and a flaming sword which turned every way, to guard the way to the tree of life" (Gen. 3:24).

Grace in the Garden

Yet there was still hope. In the midst of the curses comes blessing. First, a promise is embedded in God's curse on the serpent that one day the Seed of the woman (Christ) will crush the head of Satan (Gen. 3:15). Second, Eve would still bear children and engage in a relationship with her husband. In fact, Adam called her name Eve because "she was the mother of all living" (v. 20). Third, Adam would still be able to work, and physical death would not be immediate.

In the midst of all the losses there were also certain things Adam and Eve didn't lose. First, they didn't lose being made in the image of God. Calvin says, "Christ is the most perfect image of God; if we are conformed to it, we are so restored that with true piety, righteousness, purity, and intelligence we bear God's image.... In some part it now is manifest in the elect, in so far as they have been reborn in the spirit; but it will attain its full splendor in heaven."[3] Second, they didn't lose their identity as male and female (Gen. 1:27). The difference in the sexes is rooted in God's creation design and is not in any way destroyed by the fall. Women retain their purpose to help men in both the cultural mandate and the Great Commission. That we should be life-giving helpers is a privilege given to us

---

3. Calvin, *Institutes*, 1.15.4.

by our Creator King. Third, they didn't lose God and His word as their authority. God was still their Creator King, and His word was still His revelation of Himself to them and their rule for all of life.

Life Outside the Garden

In Genesis 4 we learn that Eve indeed experiences both the blessing and the pain of children. Her older son, Cain, killed her younger son, Abel. But the Lord gave Eve another son, Seth, and through Seth a godly line would come. In fact, it was during Seth and his son's generations that "men began to call on the name of the LORD" (Gen. 4:26).

But godly lines aren't perfect lines. The effects of the fall are seen throughout the entirety of Scripture in the lives of both believers and unbelievers. But believers have great hope. In Christ we have been reconciled to God, are freed from His wrath and curse, are able to truly enjoy life, no longer have to fear death, and no longer face an eternity of hell. In Christ we are slowly learning what it means to once again be naked and unashamed. But we are not yet what we will be. We are still often stuck in sin and shame.

Guard Your Heart

When the Lord brought His people out of Egypt, He had already proven His great redemptive love for them. But love requires obedience, and God's people didn't know all that it meant to obey God. So He gave them the Ten Commandments. The entire book of Deuteronomy, which can be thought of as Moses's greatest sermon, contains these commands, as well as many others. And one thing that is at the forefront of them all is an admonition for the people to guard their hearts.

One of the ways they were to guard their hearts was by remembering the redemption of the Lord (Deut. 4:9). In the face of idolatry, they were to seek the Lord with all their heart (v. 29). They were to take it to heart that the Lord was the only Creator King (v. 39). They were to love the Lord with all their heart (6:5). They were to remember the wilderness wanderings were tests of the heart (8:2). They were to know in their heart that the Lord's discipline was fatherly discipline (v. 5). They were warned that prosperity might bring a proud heart (v. 14). They were to fear God, walk in His ways, and serve Him with all their heart (10:12; 11:13). They were to circumcise their heart, giving it submissively to the Lord (10:16). In the face of idolatry and signs and wonders, they were to turn their heart in love toward the Lord (13:3). They were to guard their heart from unworthy thoughts that would injure their brother (15:9). The king of Israel was not to acquire many wives because they would probably turn his heart away from the Lord. He was to keep a copy of God's law and read it all the days of his life to keep a humble and pure heart (17:17–20). The people were to obey God's rules with all their heart (26:16). They were warned that exile would bring a trembling heart on them (28:65). And they were warned of turning their hearts away from the Lord to serve other gods (29:18). In other words, they were to believe God's ways were better than their ways, and His wisdom was better than their wisdom.

At the end of Deuteronomy, the Lord tells the people that they will fail to guard their hearts. They will indeed be carried into exile. But He gives them a beautiful note of grace. He will bring them back to the land and circumcise their hearts so that they will love the Lord wholeheartedly and experience a joyous life (30:1–10).

How will He do this? He will send His own Son into exile to accomplish our redemption. Christ came from heaven to earth in order to give us a new heart. Without a new heart we will always turn our hearts away from the Lord to worthless idols, believing our ways and wisdom are better than God's. But in Christ we have the capability, through the Spirit within us, to say no to the idols that so easily entangle us and yes to loving, obeying, trusting, enjoying, and serving our great God.

Hannah's Heart

On the pages of redemptive history we catch glimpses of hearts turned toward the Lord in the face of the temptation to turn them toward other things. One such heart is Hannah's. Hannah's story introduces the book of 1 Samuel, which continues Israel's history soon after the time of the judges. If there was one thing the book of Judges had revealed, it was that Israel needed a godly king. The books of 1 and 2 Samuel record for us how God raised up David, a man after God's heart, as king of Israel. But first it tells us how God established Samuel as His prophet. It was Samuel who anointed David as king of Israel (1 Sam. 16:13). As an introduction to these events, we learn of a woman named Hannah, the wife of a righteous man who faithfully worshiped the Lord. Hannah had a deep and desperate desire. She wanted children. In ancient times the ability to have children defined a woman's worth. Because children are a sign of God's great blessing (Ps. 127:3), people often viewed barrenness as a curse. A woman's family status was questionable if she didn't have children, even to the point of ostracism. This wasn't true just in Israel, but throughout the ancient Near East.[4] To make matters worse, she wasn't her husband's only wife. His other wife, Peninnah, had children. So Hannah faced great temptation to compare herself to the other woman in her husband's life and envy the children she had been given. To make matters even worse, Peninnah "provoked her severely, to make her miserable, because the LORD had closed her womb. So it was, year by year" (1 Sam. 1:6).

Things were so bad that Hannah wept and refused to eat; her heart was greatly grieved. And in the midst of it her husband couldn't understand why she was so upset, asking her, "Am I not better to you than ten sons?" (1 Sam. 1:8). But this did not pacify Hannah. Instead, in her deep distress and bitter weeping, she fell on her knees in the temple and cried out to the Lord to give her a son. In return, she would give her son to Him to be a servant in

4. John H. Walton, Victor H. Matthews, and Mark W. Chavalas, *The IVP Bible Background Commentary: Old Testament* (Downers Grove, Ill.: IVP Academic, 2000), 281–82.

the temple all his days. The priest accused Hannah of being drunk, when what she was really doing was pouring out her heart in prayer to the Lord. After Hannah explained the truth, the priest placed a blessing on her, asking the Lord to grant her request. It wasn't long before the Lord opened Hannah's womb, and she had a son named Samuel, the prophet who anointed David as king.

How was it that in the midst of deep desire, when it would have been easy to turn her heart away from the Lord, Hannah was able to turn her heart toward the Lord? How was Hannah able to recognize God's ways and wisdom were better than hers? There were two things Hannah did—she prayed and she praised. By praying we take our hearts to the Lord so that He can renew and restore them. Often our prayers are not answered in the way we ask as Hannah's was, but, regardless, prayer changes us. It realigns us with God's plans and purposes, His wisdom and ways. The heart comes saying, "Please let my will be done" and leaves saying, "Thy will be done."

But prayer wasn't the only thing Hannah did. Hannah also praised the Lord. She recognized His salvation, holiness, kingship, strength, knowledge, justice, power, sovereignty, protection of His children, and judgment. Hannah could give Peninnah's taunts, her husband's questioning, and Samuel to the Lord because her heart was renewed and refocused in prayer and praise. She exchanged her ways and wisdom for His. In the midst of strong desires, we must do the same. We must turn to prayer and praise in order to have a healthy heart.

Michal's Heart

In stark contrast to Hannah in the same book (in the Hebrew Bible, the English 1 and 2 Samuel is just one book), we meet another woman, Michal. Michal was Saul's daughter and had been given to David as his wife, but Michal's heart was not turned in the right direction. She believed that her ways and wisdom were better than the Lord's. When David came to Jerusalem with the ark of the Lord, leaping and dancing, "she despised him in her heart" (2 Sam. 6:16). Instead of holding David in honor as the Lord's anointed king, Michal did not find him worthy. While David turned toward prayer and praise, as Hannah did, Michal rejected these actions. Scripture ends the story of Michal on this somber note: "Michal the daughter of Saul had no child to the day of her death" (v. 23). The unhealthy heart harbors contempt where there should be adoration; the healthy heart expresses adoration where there could be contempt. The unhealthy heart is filled with worldly wisdom and ways; the healthy heart is turned toward God's wisdom and ways.

Who Can Understand the Heart?

How do we know whether our hearts are healthy or unhealthy? How do we know if we are turned toward God's wisdom and ways or worldly wisdom and ways? Many of us are familiar with Psalm 1, which contrasts the righteous man with the rebellious, but there is a similar passage in Jeremiah 17, the context of which is the Lord indicting Judah for its sin. It is another of those diagnostic tests in Scripture that reveals our lovers. Who or what has captured our heart, and why? Jeremiah writes,

> Cursed is the man who trusts in man
> And makes flesh his strength,
> Whose heart departs from the LORD.
> For he shall be like a shrub in the desert....
>
> Blessed is the man who trusts in the LORD....
> He shall be like a tree planted by the waters....
>
> The heart is deceitful above all things,
> And desperately wicked;
> Who can know it?
> I, the LORD, search the heart,
> I test the mind. (vv. 5–10)

Too many times I have trusted man (either myself or another person) and made flesh my strength, which means my heart has turned away from the Lord to have my satisfaction or security met in other things. What happens when we do this is comparable to a shrub in the desert, which is far from beautiful and fruitful. But when we trust in the Lord, we become like a tree planted by water with no fear of heat or anxiousness for drought. We never cease to bear fruit.

It is only in Christ that this can happen. The imagery of a tree and bearing fruit is picked up in John 15. Apart from Christ we can do nothing, but in Christ we bear much fruit and prove that we are truly Christ's disciples (vv. 5, 8). Trusting in man brings fear and anxiety, but trusting in Christ brings faith and fruitfulness, adoration and affection. It is this faith and fruitfulness, adoration and affection, that yield a heart set on God's wisdom and ways.

Naked and Bare

Yet Scripture makes it clear that we often fall far short of faith and fruitfulness, adoration and affection. Ezekiel 16 is one of the most scandalous and shocking pictures of our salvation in Scripture. It begins with the sobering reality that Jerusalem is a faithless bride. The Lord reminds His people that their origin and birth were of pagans. No one had compassion on them at birth; instead, they were cast off into an open field. When the Lord saw Israel, He gave life to her and "made [her] thrive like a plant in the field; and [she] grew, matured, and became very beautiful. [Her] breasts were formed, [her] hair grew, but [she was] naked and bare" (v. 7).

At the age of love, the Lord covered her nakedness and entered into a covenant with her, taking her as His bride. He made her "exceedingly beautiful" and advanced her to royalty (Ezek. 16:13). She was renowned around the world because of her beauty. She was perfectly beautiful because the Lord bestowed splendor on her. But she trusted in her beauty instead of trusting in the Lord and was faithless to Him. She exchanged God's wisdom and ways for her own wisdom and ways. She gave her beauty to anyone who passed by her from other nations. "And in all [her] abominations and acts of harlotry [she] did not remember the days of [her] youth, when [she was] naked and bare" (v. 22). The Lord says, "How degenerate is your heart!...

seeing you do all these things, the deeds of a brazen harlot…. Yet you were not like a harlot, because you scorned payment. You are an adulterous wife, who takes strangers instead of her husband" (vv. 30–32). The Lord gathers her lovers against her in order to uncover her nakedness to them and judge her for committing adultery. He gives her into their hands, and they take her beauty and leave her naked and bare (v. 39).

Amazingly, the chapter doesn't end with judgment. Instead, the Lord remembers His covenant: "'And I will establish My covenant with you. Then you shall know that I am the LORD, that you may remember and be ashamed, and never open your mouth anymore because of your shame, when I provide you an atonement for all you have done,' says the Lord GOD" (Ezek. 16:62–63).

Clearly the days of being naked and unashamed were long gone. Like Adam and Eve, Jerusalem had been crowned with true beauty. The Lord had made her beautiful. Yet instead of recognizing this beauty as His gift of grace, she trusted in it and then gave it away. Instead of recognizing His wisdom and ways, she trusted in her own. As soon as she did this, she became naked and ashamed before her lovers. Don't miss what her lovers did—they stole her beauty and left her naked and bare; they ruined her reputation; and then they killed her (Ezek. 16:39–41).

True beauty is found only in Christ. Giving ourselves to any other lover—an idol—leaves us naked and ashamed. False lovers wreck our lives, ruin our reputations, and ravage the life within us. This passage gives us tremendous hope. False lovers don't have the final word. Jesus Christ came to make our sick hearts well and to atone for every time we have exchanged, continue to exchange, or will exchange our covenant Lord for other lovers with whom we take pleasure.

Liberty to the Captives

Christ came to set us free from our worldly wisdom and ways. Can you imagine what it would have been like for the people in the synagogue who heard Jesus read from the scroll of Isaiah? He proclaimed He was the fulfillment of these words:

> The Spirit of the LORD is upon Me,
> Because He has anointed Me
> To preach the gospel to the poor;
> He has sent Me to heal the brokenhearted,
> To proclaim liberty to the captives,
> And recovery of sight to the blind,
> To set at liberty those who are oppressed;
> To proclaim the acceptable year of the LORD.
> (Luke 4:18–19)

This verse was pregnant with meaning for those acquainted with the Old Testament. This was the Year of Jubilee! The book of Leviticus tells us that it is a year of release (25:8–22). Slaves were released from servitude. Debtors were released from debt. And landowners were released from having lost property—it was given back to them. Jesus's proclamation of the year of the Lord's favor was the greatest that Israel had ever known. Jesus had come to set free those enslaved to sin, to release sinners from their debt of sin, and to restore paradise lost to its rightful owners, the elect of God.

These verses are filled with hope for those of us who feel captive to the addictions that beset us, blind to truth, and oppressed by sin and shame. We need the Lord to set us free, and these verses remind us that not only can He set us free, He does. His mission never fails among God's people. If we are His, then He has good news for us. No longer do we have to be poor, captive, blind, and oppressed. No longer do we have to follow our own wisdom or our own ways. We can know the riches of Christ, enjoy His freedom, see truth clearly, and understand what it means to be liberated from that which enslaves us. But is it really that easy? Don't we have to do something?

Setting of Our Hearts

In his letter to the saints at Colossae, the apostle Paul spent the first half telling them who Christ is and what He had done for them. With these facts as the foundation, he turned to the commands in the second half of his letter. In other words, he is saying something like this: Now that you know how much Christ loves you and all that He has done for you, this then is how you should live. This is how heart change happens. This is how you stop trusting in your own ways and your own wisdom and start trusting in Christ's. As we learn more of who Christ is and more of what He has done for us, our hearts will be set on things above, in the heavenly places where Christ reigns, instead of on earthly things where the world, the devil, and our own flesh tempt us to sin.

Colossians 3 addresses how to set our hearts toward seeking things that are above.

First, know who you are. The old man has died; we are a new creation in Christ. United to Him, we have His Spirit's power at work within us. Second, know what is earthly in you. We need to recognize that we are prone to sexual immorality, impurity, passion, evil desires, covetousness, idolatry, anger, wrath, malice, slander, obscene talk, and lying. We need to call sin, sin and recognize these things deserve God's wrath. Third, know what you need to put on as God's chosen people who have the power of the Holy Spirit within them. We need to strive to put on compassionate hearts, kindness, humility, meekness, patience, forgiveness, love, peace, and thankfulness. Finally, know truth, teach truth, sing truth, and act on truth. If the word of God doesn't dwell in us, we will believe the words of the world, the devil, and our flesh. The heart set on things above is the heart that knows its identity is in Christ, recognizes its sinfulness, believes God's power is sufficient to put on a heart of love, and strives to know, teach, sing, and act on truth. It is the heart that sings of God's wisdom and God's ways.

I know I'm not the only one who has suffered from a poor body image. I have prayed for and counseled others through high school, college, seminary, and all my single and married life. One thing I have learned is that a degree, career, boyfriend, or marriage doesn't solve body image problems. But the gospel does. And so I hope that throughout the pages of this book you will be encouraged, edified, educated, and equipped. I pray you will learn how deeply this problem affects women, be reminded that our body image must come from Scripture alone, and have renewed hope that in Christ we are accepted not on our appearance, but on Christ's active and passive obedience.

THINKING ABOUT THESE THINGS

1. Describe a time when you have felt naked and ashamed.

2. What have you learned in this chapter about why we feel naked and ashamed?

3. How did Hannah's story affect your thinking about your present heart's desire?

4. Contrast Hannah's heart with Michal's. When have you recently yielded to God's ways and wisdom, and when have you recently relied on your own ways and wisdom?

5. What did you learn from Ezekiel 16 about false
   lovers versus your true lover, the Lord God?

6. How does Luke 4:18–19 apply to body image battles?

7. What did you learn from Colossians 3 about how to
   turn your heart toward the Lord?

8. Spend time in prayer today using Psalm 139. Slowly
   read it out loud. How do the words challenge you?
   Convict you? Comfort you? Change you?

Chapter 2

Mirror, Mirror, on the Wall

In kindergarten I was a head taller than everyone else in my class, including the boys. By the time I was a freshman in high school I was six feet two. One of my friends called me Raffe (short for giraffe), and another friend called me Shorty. It wasn't uncommon for me to hear a child say to his or her mother, "Look at how big that girl is" as she smiled apologetically at me. I always wondered why the child couldn't have said "tall" instead of "big." I would sometimes be asked, "Do you model?" and frequently, "Do you play basketball?" I was a tall, slender girl who tried to carry myself well, but I was self-conscious about my height. When I was thirteen years old, I wrote in my prayer journal:

Lord, please help me to get through all the name-calling of Tree and Beanpole, and help me to find myself, and to be a wonderful Christian. Lord, I've always wanted to be the perfect person—blonde hair, blue eyes, nice body for my boyfriend, good friend, but Lord, I see now I can't have it all, and I realize I rely too much on myself to become a good Christian when I really need the guidance of my holy Father.

During my teenage years, I always saw billboards that depicted beauty as having a slender, picture-perfect body. Every grocery store had a row of magazines screaming, "You have to look like 'her' in order to be beautiful!" At the age of fourteen I wrote:

I know I should be patient [for a boyfriend], but sometimes I want one because everyone else always seems to have one. I'm either always too tall, or too shy, or not pretty enough, or so it seems. I know God made me in His own likeness, but it sure is hard to remember that when you're judged by the world so much.

At the age of seventeen I sought forgiveness for making comparisons:

Forgive me for comparing myself to others rather than knowing that You formed and shaped me exactly the way You desired.

You can see that I was already battling the lies of this world, particularly "You have to look like 'her' in order to be beautiful or loved," with the truth of God's Word, but the battle was strong, and it would prove to be long.

A Carnival Mirror

Have you ever had the experience of looking in a fun house mirror? The mirror distorts your image so that you appear differently from how you really are. One company that sells them boasts their product is "simple, safe and fun." For me, though, every mirror seemed to be a carnival mirror. And they were anything but simple, safe, and fun. When I looked at myself in them, whether in my own home, a dressing room, or a public restroom, what I saw was distorted. Even though I was slender, I thought I was fat. Even though I was, according to many, a beautiful young girl, I couldn't see myself that way. I saw flaws instead of a figure that God had created for His glory.

What I needed was a different mirror. I needed to stop looking at myself critically and go to the Word of God, which is perfect and beautiful. James calls it the "law of liberty" (James 1:25), and indeed it is. When we learn truth from God's Word, we are liberated from the distortion we see in the mirrors on our walls. No longer do we need to hear the mirror say that we are the prettiest of them all. In Christ, all of us are beautiful. There is no room for competition at the foot of the cross. He has taken ugly sinners and made beautiful saints. Our beauty comes from Him, and it is a beauty that, instead of fading, grows increasingly greater until we see Him face-to-face (1 Cor. 13:12). We don't have to look like "her" in order to be loved. God loved us when we weren't pretty at all. We were dead in our trespasses and sins, walking according to the world's wisdom and ways. But God loved us enough to save us so that He can make us into the image of His Son (Eph. 2:1–10).

A Weighty Scale

It wasn't just the mirror that wasn't simple, safe, and fun. It was also the scale. I had a love-hate relationship with my scale. When my number was where I wanted it to be, I loved it. When my number wasn't, I hated it. I would weigh myself regularly, forgetting the ebb and flow of weight fluctuation relative to how much water I had drunk or what time of day I weighed in. All I was concerned about was the "right number." This was a weighty expectation to live under. I was enslaved to an object that sat on my bathroom floor. Its number defined me, and it either depressed me or delighted me.

The problem wasn't with the scale, but with my perception of its significance. You would have thought that instead of a number it had words: "not thin enough," "too fat," "keep working," "you have a ways to go," "imperfect," or "unlovely." Eventually I got rid of it, recognizing it was a trigger for me in my addiction to thinness and fitness. This was one of the best choices I made. Even at the doctor's office, I would ask the nurse to write down my weight without telling me. It had become a snare to an improper evaluation of my significance, and I wanted nothing to do with it. Even today I say a quick prayer before the doctor tells me my weight: "Lord, please help me remember this number doesn't define me." Sometimes I simply ask them not to tell me. And I've never brought a scale back into my bathroom. I don't want the temptation to be there.

I needed a different kind of scale than the one on my bathroom floor. Instead of planting my feet on an object

in order to define my beauty, I needed to plant my feet
on the sure foundation of Christ, my rock and my salvation. He doesn't define our worth by a number, but by His
nail-pierced hands. We are so beautiful in His eyes that He
came and sought us, then bought us, in order to make us
what we ought to be.

Unlike King Belshazzar of Babylon, we will never be
weighed in the balances and found wanting (Dan. 5:27).
Those of us in Christ will never be weighed for our significance. He has scaled the wall of salvation for us, taken
God's wrath and curse, and obeyed the law perfectly. Therefore, "let us lay aside every weight, and the sin which so
easily ensnares us, and let us run with endurance the race
that is set before us, looking unto Jesus, the author and finisher of our faith, who for the joy that was set before Him
endured the cross, despising the shame, and has sat down
at the right hand of the throne of God" (Heb. 12:1–2).

Beauty Billboards and Seductive Centerfolds
It wasn't just the mirror and the scale that tempted me
to believe I wasn't pretty enough or thin enough. Every
trip down the highway gave me another lesson in beauty
according to this world. Whether it was billboards adver-
tising plastic surgery, diet pills, or adult stores, the message
was plain. Beauty consists in the perfect body and in being
sexually appealing. In other words, "You have to look like
'her' in order to be beautiful in a man's eyes."

Trips through grocery stores were another lesson. Lin-
ing the shelves at the checkout counter were reminders

that I was to be thin, sexy, and perfectly manicured to be lovely. Again, the lie that was slowly taking root in my young heart was, "You have to look like 'her' to be loved." That was a hopeless thought. Who can live up to images that are airbrushed to perfection? Who can do their own hair like a top designer every day? Who can apply their own makeup as well as a professional makeup artist? It seemed like a losing battle to me, and that was both discouraging and depressing.

I began to learn that I had to bounce my eyes off of these billboards and magazines. I was battling the sin of comparison and covetousness. It is not that I wanted to be sexually provocative, but I did want to be beautiful, even in the eyes of the world. And I found myself comparing my body to the bodies of women on the covers of magazines. So I had to learn to bounce my eyes—look away. I still do this when I'm near billboards and magazine racks or even around women at the pool, the mall, or church—anywhere that I'm tempted to compare my body to another woman's I redirect my eyes. I don't want to compare or covet; that is sin.

Now that I'm a mother of both boys and girls, I often have conversations with my children about the magazines at checkout counters or the billboards on the highway. Before we go into the store or pass the billboard, I remind them to bounce their eyes and why it is important to do so. If I know where magazines are placed throughout the store or where the billboards are on the highway, I'll warn my children of their location. I pray for my children's purity, as well as my husband's and my own, wanting all of us to have a biblical view of beauty and sexuality and a heart of purity.

Likes and Comments

With the explosion of social media, particularly Instagram, women today are facing the same temptation of finding their self-worth in a new and pervasive way: in other people's comments about them, in the number of likes they receive on a Facebook post, or in how many people retweet what they post. Posting pictures and seeing how many people don't like your new hairstyle or dress has been the downfall into depression of many women. On the other hand, likes and comments such as "You're beautiful" may make you feel good for a moment, but there is no lasting fulfillment in other people's perceptions of us. They don't place a value on us; God does.

Sarah's Daughters

If there had been social media during Abraham's day, surely his wife would have received many likes for her appearance. Sarai was beautiful. In fact, Sarai's beauty actually endangered her. Abraham was afraid to tell the Egyptians that she was his wife because he thought the Egyptians would kill him so they could keep her (Gen. 12:11–20). But for all her beauty, Sarai had no child, and as we learned in the last chapter, barrenness in the ancient Near East was seen as the opposite of blessing (Ps. 127:3). It is likely that Sarai felt worthless. She actually gave her servant to her husband so that she could obtain an heir through her, but when Hagar conceived, she felt contempt for Sarai, and Sarai was filled with anger and dealt harshly with Hagar (Gen. 16:1–6).

About thirteen years later, the Lord changed Sarai's name to Sarah, which means "princess," and God promised her a son—indeed, a family line filled with nations and kings of people (Gen. 17:15–16). By this time Sarah was old and had probably given up the idea of ever having a child of her own. She laughed in disbelief at the idea of it all (18:12). But God wasn't kidding; His promises are faithful and true.

In God's perfect timing Sarah conceived. Sarah and Abraham named their son Isaac, which means "laughter" (Gen. 21:1–3, 6). For all the external beauty that Sarah had, her life didn't look very beautiful to the eyes that don't see by faith. But the author of Hebrews commends her, "By faith Sarah herself also received strength to conceive seed, and she bore a child when she was past the age, because she judged Him faithful who had promised" (11:11). In exhorting the wives among his readers not to let their adorning be external, but internal, Peter uses Sarah as an example of one who adorned herself with submission to her own husband (1 Peter 3:3–6). Although the Genesis account gives us every reason to believe Sarah could have boasted in her external beauty, the New Testament commends her for her faith in God and her faithfulness to her husband. The world tells us our beauty is found in our hairstyles, jewelry, figures, and clothing, but God's Word tells us beauty is found in a godly heart (v. 4).

A Gentle and Quiet Spirit

When my oldest daughter was in fourth grade, she began sharing with me things that were said to her or around her that defined beauty according to this world. Makeup, nail polish, fashionable clothing, and firm abs were a few things she mentioned. In each conversation Hannah had to choose whether she was going to believe that these things defined her beauty. These stories gave us the opportunity to speak of beauty in the world's eyes versus beauty in the Lord's eyes. I want my daughters to know the truth so that they can be discerning when they hear different definitions of beauty around them. And I hope you want your daughters or granddaughters to know too. Some of you reading this book are young professionals who are not married and don't have children. You also have the opportunity to mentor these younger girls, helping them define beauty according to God's Word instead of the world.

God's Word says, "Do not let your adornment be merely outward—arranging the hair, wearing gold, or putting on fine apparel; rather let it be the hidden person of the heart, with the incorruptible beauty of a gentle and quiet spirit, which is very precious in the sight of God" (1 Peter 3:3–4). These verses are so important to informing our definition of beauty in the face of the world, the devil, and our own flesh. Notice what Peter does not say. He doesn't say to stop arranging our hair, wearing jewelry, or putting on nice clothes. What he says is, "Don't let that be your beauty." In other words, do those things for the glory of God (1 Cor. 10:31), but don't think you are beautiful because of those things. Slow down and let that truth transform your thinking for a moment. This is against everything we've been taught since we were little girls. We are not to define our beauty by what others (or we) see. When people compliment our hair, jewelry, or clothing, we should not tuck that away in the "I'm beautiful" category. Similarly, when people don't compliment our hair, jewelry, or clothing, we shouldn't conclude, "I'm not beautiful." This is a very freeing truth! Beauty, according to God's Word, comes from the heart. This means that we must take the time to arrange, adorn, and clothe our hearts even more than we take the time to arrange our hair, put on our jewelry, and put on nice clothes.

We don't do this in order to be beautiful before the Lord. We are already beautiful to Him because Christ has given us His beauty. But because we are beautiful, and because we know that one day Christ will claim His people as His bride, we strive now to be what one day we will be—"a glorious church, not having spot or wrinkle or any such thing, but…holy and without blemish" (Eph. 5:27). So we are to arrange our hearts toward holiness and godliness. We are to adorn our hearts with Christ so that we don't fulfill the lusts of our flesh (Rom. 13:14). And we are to clothe ourselves with humility so that we might experience the grace of God (1 Peter 5:5). Such a beauty regime surely makes the beauty of this world pale in comparison. Isn't it true that the women you know who are most holy and godly are also the people you find to be the most beautiful? We need to stop defining our beauty by the mirror, the scale, the billboards, and the magazines, and define our beauty by our heart.

A Tale of Two Wives

Defining our beauty by our heart is difficult to do in a world focused on external beauty, a trend that is as old as Genesis. Genesis 29 provides us with one example. Jacob couldn't take his eyes off of Rachel. She was beautiful, and he was willing to work seven long years to have her as his wife (v. 18). What a surprise, then, when he woke to find Rachel's sister, Leah, instead of Rachel lying next to him (v. 25). Leah was not known for her external beauty. In fact, her beauty is set in contrast with her sister's: "Leah's eyes were delicate, but Rachel was beautiful of form and appearance" (v. 17). To make matters worse, Jacob was angry with his father-in-law for deceiving him and said, "Was it not for Rachel that I served you?" (v. 25). So after Jacob fulfilled the customary wedding week with Leah, his father-in-law also gave him Rachel as his wife, and Jacob "loved Rachel more than Leah" (v. 30).

Scripture doesn't give us Leah's detailed response as she suffered as "second best" or "the ugly sister" for many years. But we have a good idea of how she responded by the way she named her children, and we have a good idea of how the Lord looks upon the unloved of this world in His response of blessing Leah with children. Remember that infertility in ancient times was comparable to worthlessness. So in this story of the two wives, our hearts go out to both Rachel, who remains barren while Leah is very fruitful, as well as to Leah, who remains unlovely and unloved while Rachel is lovely and loved.

Leah named her first child Reuben ("a son") because "the LORD has surely looked on my affliction. Now therefore, my husband will love me" (Gen. 29:32). With eyes of faith she believed the Lord had seen her affliction and given her a son to make her lovely in Jacob's eyes. Yet at the same time, by seeking significance in her husband's love for her, she was falling prey to a lie we'll look at in the next chapter—that our significance is found in whether or not a man loves us. She named her second son Simeon ("heard") "because the LORD has heard that I am unloved, He has therefore given me this son also" (v. 33). Again, she believed the Lord was intimately acquainted with her unfavorable circumstances and was at work in the midst of them. Seeking significance in her husband's love for her, Leah named her third son Levi ("attached"), saying, "Now this time my husband will become attached to me, because I have borne him three sons" (v. 34). She named her fourth son Judah ("praise"), saying, "Now I will praise the LORD" (v. 35).

How do you think beautiful Rachel felt about unloved and unlovely Leah as she watched her bear these four children while she remained barren? Genesis 30:1 tells us, "Rachel envied her sister, and said to Jacob, 'Give me children, or else I die!'" This response reflects the lie we'll look at in chapter 5—that if we had what "she" has we would be satisfied, secure, and significant.

When Leah thought she had stopped bearing children, she gave her maid to Jacob to be his wife. Because the sons born to her maid were considered hers, she named them, and we continue to learn about Leah's heart from the name she gives especially to the second of the two sons her maid bore for her. She named him Asher ("happy") because, she said, "I am happy, for the daughters will call me blessed" (Gen. 30:13). Here again we see Leah placing her significance in someone other than the Lord.

Then the Lord opened Leah's womb again and she bore Jacob two more sons, Issachar and Zebulun ("dwelling"), meaning, "God has endowed me with a good endowment; now my husband will dwell with me, because I have borne him six sons" (Gen. 30:20). Although Leah recognized God's good gift to her in Zebulun, at the same time she believed the lie that her worth came from her ability (or performance) to have six sons for her husband.

The only other book in Scripture Leah is mentioned in is in the book of Ruth, but what is said about her is significant. Immediately after Boaz acquired Ruth to be his wife and just before the wedding day, the people and elders of the city pronounced a blessing on the happy couple: "The LORD make the woman who is coming to your house like Rachel and Leah, the two who built the house of Israel" (Ruth 4:11). Here Leah takes her place alongside Rachel as a colaborer to build the people of God. We know that God built the house of Israel using imperfect people like Rachel and Leah. Through their story we learn that the Lord, unlike Jacob, loves the unlovely and takes us to be His own. But note here that despite their flaws (and they had many), they were women of faith. There is no mention of

Rachel's beautiful form or Leah's weak eyes; their legacy for generations to come was that God used them to build the house of Israel. And it was through the line of Leah's son Judah that Jesus Christ would come. Because Leah looked to God in faith, though imperfectly and often believing lies about her beauty and worth, she was able to praise God even when she was unlovely and unloved in Jacob's eyes. It was this Leah whom the Lord graciously used to bring forth the line of Judah from which Christ came.

Beauty Is Vain

The story of Rachel and Leah isn't the only portion of Scripture that teaches external beauty is fruitless. As I look back over my lifetime I see how true Proverbs 31:30 is: "Charm is deceitful and beauty is passing, but a woman who fears the LORD, she shall be praised." When I was a teenager I was focused on having a thin, fit, beautiful body so that a man would love me. But I was chasing after a beauty that was fleeting. If you are a young woman chasing after these things, I plead with you to stop. Or maybe you are a young mother and you've realized that you will never again have your teenage or prepregnancy body back. Tummy tucks, breast enhancements, nose jobs, wax jobs, and antiaging creams cannot keep us from growing old. That is why beauty is vain. But Scripture tells us what isn't vain and what we should be spending our time and days doing. We are to fear the Lord. If you are an older woman in the church who has learned the value of fearing the Lord instead of fearing your image in the mirror, please help younger women understand it too. The younger generations need the older ones to redefine beauty for them in a biblical way. We don't have to look like "her" to be loved. We are already loved and beautiful in Christ. And as those who are beautiful in Him, we are to honor Him by recognizing that His wisdom and His ways are best.

Proverbs 1:7 says, "The fear of the LORD is the beginning of knowledge, but fools despise wisdom and instruction." In Scripture fearing the Lord is related to obeying His commands (Deut. 5:29), serving Him (Deut. 10:20), knowing and worshiping His name (Ps. 22:23), trusting Him (Pss. 23:4; 115:11), enjoying a relationship with Him (Ps. 25:14), experiencing His provision and protection (Pss. 27:3; 111:5), turning away from evil (Prov. 3:7; 16:6), enjoying an abundant life (Prov. 10:27; 19:23), having wealth (Prov. 15:16; 22:4), gaining wisdom (Prov. 15:33), experiencing His mercy (Luke 1:50), and giving Him glory (Rev. 14:7). These things are to occupy our time and attention, not the mirror on our wall, the scale in our bathroom, or others' comments about us. The book of Ecclesiastes was written by King Solomon, who knew power, position, and prestige very well. It is significant that the book opens with, "Vanity of vanities, all is vanity" (Eccl. 1:2) and closes with, "Fear God and keep His commandments, for this is man's all" (12:13).

I'm not sure you'll be able to relate to sticking out in a
crowd because you are six feet two, but maybe you stick
out in other ways, and maybe that has made you self-
conscious about your body. Perhaps your definition of
beauty has been more informed by the world and your
own flesh than you would like to admit. Thankfully, the
Word of God defines beauty for us. It is the beauty of the
heart that is turned to the Lord in adoration and affection,
fear and faith, love and longing, wonder and worship. The
woman who fears the Lord will be praised.

THINKING ABOUT THESE THINGS

1. How do you view your reflection in the mirror or
   your weight on a scale?

2. How have billboards, magazines, and social media
   affected you with regard to comparing yourself to
   other women or coveting their beauty? When have
   you been tempted to believe the lie that you have to
   look like "her" in order to be beautiful?

3. How does the story of Sarah encourage you?

4. What does it mean to have "a gentle and quiet spirit"?

5. What thoughts did you take away from the story of
   Rachel and Leah?

6. Spend time in prayer and praise today, especially with regard to a situation the Lord redeemed when the world or your family thought you "less than" someone else.

7. Reflect on Proverbs 31:30 and the verses associated with fearing the Lord. Choose one to meditate on this week.

Chapter 3

Longing for Love

I started liking boys when I was in fifth grade. In our school classroom there were notes that would circulate asking, "Will you go with me?" and you had to check the yes or no box. I remember feeling pressure to receive one of those notes. It felt like a popularity contest on which my worth depended. I longed to be liked and for a boy to write a note to me, and when he did, it felt good. I was smitten with a boy named Oliver, as you can see from my first love poem:

His soft blond hair blows softly in the breeze,
His eyes sparkle when he talks to me.
His smile warms my heart every day
And lovely thoughts swarm around me.
I know he cares and
He's always willing to share things with me.

Without realizing it, in fifth grade I was already beginning to buy into the lie that my worth was based on whether I received attention from a boy. This search for security and significance from a relationship would prove to be a theme throughout my tweens, teens, and early twenties.

First Kiss

When I was in seventh grade, one of the eighth-grade boys in my youth group asked me on a double date. At one point during the evening, he quickly turned and kissed me. That was the first time a boy had kissed me. Although I wasn't expecting it, it made me feel like someone special.

In ninth grade my date from homecoming kissed me in front of my peers at a party. My friends noticed, and their words to me affirmed I was a lucky and popular girl that evening. It made me feel good that they accepted me as a girl who was beautiful, popular, and wanted, and it made me feel good to have a boy affirm my beauty by kissing me. Toward the end of my senior year and just in time for prom, I dated a young man in my youth group. Once again it felt good to have a boy affirm my beauty by pursuing me in a relationship. During my middle school and high school years, I had slowly and subtly bought into the lie that I was beautiful if a boy pursued me.

Passion and Purity

I began praying for my future husband when I was still in high school, so when I got to college my eyes were wide open for the Lord's answer. Without realizing it, I had equated marriage with my significance and worth. Because purity was also a huge desire for me, I wasn't interested in a short-term relationship but in a godly relationship that would eventually lead to marriage. At age seventeen I wrote:

> Father, because I am yet pure and a virgin I desire You to keep me that way until You give me a godly man to marry and I can honorably give myself to him. I pray that I will resist all temptations that come to me before then. Help me to be holy and pure, Lord. Father, I pray for a man who is godly and pure in my life, Lord. To keep something such as my virginity for my husband is my desire, and I desire for him to keep his virginity for me.

Throughout the course of my college and seminary years, I dated five different Christian men. Because we were dating to discover if marriage was right for us, we struggled with passion and purity. We kissed more than we should have. We crossed emotional boundaries we should not have crossed. If I could do it over again, I would. And if you, dear reader, have regrets too, I want you to know that there is forgiveness at the foot of the cross. When we come to our heavenly Father in repentance, He forgives us.

When I didn't have a boyfriend, I struggled with loneliness and insecurity. I was more prone to believe that I wasn't beautiful or significant when I wasn't dating a man. At age nineteen I wrote,

> In these despairing moments of loneliness when my heart gets weighed down, You continue to wrap Your loving arms around me.

At the age of twenty-one, I allowed my heart and fears to get in the way of letting go of a long relationship with my best friend, whom I had dated off and on for three years. I was headed to seminary hundreds of miles away, and I was afraid our relationship might get in the way of what the Lord had planned for me there. I enjoyed the times he said, "I love you" and the gifts and hugs he gave me. I wondered if there would be anyone else out there for me. I was scared to let go of him and face loneliness. I didn't know how to do it—or even if the Lord wanted me to do it:

> To feel the ache of sacrificial love—loving someone means leaving them solely to you to do with what you want. Nothing thus far has been quite so hard as surrendering an earthly love. Sometimes I wonder if I can bear to let go of him, but then I remember who I'm letting go of him for and I'm reminded of your great mercy and love and comforting arms. Let him be material for sacrifice, Father. Accept him as a gift offering to you. Take my will and conform it to yours.

While I was at seminary, I wrote this to my future husband:

> Oh where are you? Do you long for me as I long for you?...
>
> Oh, wait for me! One day our Lord will majestically bring us together!
>
> Our hearts will beat as one. Our lives will piece together.

Our eyes will meet, our hands clasp, our lips touch, and love will be awakened in us as we've never known before.

Wait, wait for me, wait for Him—He's working.

Since I had been in several serious relationships during my college and early seminary years, I felt convicted that I needed a time to focus solely on the Lord:

Be gracious to me, O God, according to Your lovingkindness; according to the greatness of Your compassion blot out my memories of past transgressions in relationships.... For I know now what I did was harmful and not glorifying to You—what I thought were okay boundaries were really not, and my past is ever before me. Against You I defiled Your place of residing. My sinful nature is prone to such passion, but as Your child, You desire truth and purity in the innermost being. Purify me with hyssop, Lord, and I shall be clean; wash me, and I shall be whiter than snow.

This time of focusing solely on the Lord was not as long as I expected. A Christian man was interested in dating me, and after seeking counsel from one of my mentors at seminary, I said yes. But eventually I determined our ministry paths weren't aligned, and I broke up with him when I was twenty-three, an age I thought I would have already been married. I wrote:

Jesus, lover of my soul, draw me close to Thee
I know no other longing than the one I have for Thee....

I'll follow your leading, I'll follow your call
At costs of all others forsake them, stand tall
I'll follow my master where He leadeth me
Through highlands and parched lands, wherever we be
I'll allege to no other, for You are the one
My Savior, my Master who did bid me come
Come not for the comfort nor stress-free days
But come for the glory of that great kingdom day.

Here Comes the Bride

After graduating from seminary, I accepted my first ministry position near my parents' home. I lived with them for a few months before I, a single woman, purchased my first house. This was hard for me. I always thought I would purchase a home with my husband. How my heart ached at the string of broken hearts I had left behind me. Was I right to break up with them? After all, they were godly men. I questioned if I should have let them go. That longing for marriage was still burning within me. Would the right man ever come along? Why were these godly men never enough for me?

Through each of those relationships the Lord was slowly revealing to me that my satisfaction, security, and significance must be found in Him alone, not in a man. Up to that point I really wasn't ready to get married. The Lord was still at work in my heart, rooting out lies that I had so easily believed. I had become dependent on a man to feel worthy. The Lord wanted me to know I was already worthy in Him. These men hadn't been enough for me because they couldn't fill the hole in my heart that Christ alone can fill. The problem wasn't so much in the man but in the expectations I had for the man.

In God's sovereign and providential plan, my future husband worked down the street from the church where I worked. We had known each other since I was in high school and had attended the same church. In fact, he had taken me, as a friend, to my junior homecoming. He was afraid to ruin our friendship, but not so afraid that he wasn't willing to risk it, so while we sat together on a pew in the church where I served as the assistant director of women's ministry, he asked if he could pursue me toward marriage. I wrote:

> Father, I acknowledge to you my deep desire for marriage and thus my vulnerability right now in dating. I pray that you would lead and guide—even my friendship with Charles right now—and that you would guard my heart. You are my first love. I don't need anyone or anything else to be complete.

Two months later, on that same pew, Charles proposed. And five months later, in the same sanctuary, we got married:

> Chosen as your bride-to-be
> Held in peace by Divine Sovereignty
> All of the days that stretch ahead
> Relishing one another with God as our stead
> Loving you passionately, tenderly, in a servant way

Enveloped by the ecstasy of love's glorious sway
Secrets shared by lovers to whisper in your ears
Even so, there will be times you'll wipe away my tears
Drawing me close to you, holding me tight
Witnessing times I need to see Christ's light
Allowing me freedom to reach and to grow
Releasing me to the fields ripe so I can sow
Deeply we'll fall into covenant love
Imbibing deeply with our source being God up above
Valiant warrior you are to me
Incredible knight, this I see
Living for His glory in marriage I pray
Looking to Him for guidance each day.

While you may or may not relate to the details of my story, you can probably relate to the temptation to believe that your worth is defined by whether or not a man loves you. Over the twenty-plus years I've spent ministering to women, it has been my experience that their struggles today are often struggles of yesterday. Women, like me, who were tempted to find their significance, worth, and beauty in their relationship with men in their younger years are still tempted to do so, but in different ways. This is true regardless of whether we are married or single, although it manifests itself differently. For example, some of my single friends are tempted to define their worth by the circumstance that no man has pursued them toward marriage. The dreams for marriage that they had in their earlier years seem to be slipping away, and they are tempted to conclude they are not beautiful enough or good enough for a man to want to marry them. For me, as a married woman, I sometimes feel anger and disappointment when my husband doesn't celebrate a special occasion with me as I wish he would. When I examine my heart, I realize that I still believe the old lie that my beauty and worth are defined by a man's love for me, and he evidently doesn't think I'm beautiful or worthy enough to plan something special for me. No husband will be able to meet these expectations, nor should he. Christ alone gives us our significance.

Abigail, a Woman of Discretion and Beauty

There is a woman we learn about in 1 Samuel 25 who could have believed that her worth was dependent on her husband, but instead she looked to the Lord. Abigail was married to a very wealthy businessman, but he was harsh, and his behavior was hideous (vv. 2–3). Nabal was so harsh and hideous that he didn't treat David's young men well when they requested provision for themselves and David on a feast day (vv. 10–11). Since Nabal rudely refused David's request, David and his men strapped on their swords and prepared to teach Nabal a lesson (v. 13). One of the young men who served Nabal and Abigail's household told Abigail what was happening (vv. 14–17).

Abigail quickly did what was right. She prepared what David had asked for and sent it on ahead of her with her young men. Then she followed. When she met David, she bowed in humble submission and respect before him. She minced no words and hid nothing from David. She admitted her husband was a fool. She asked forgiveness for not seeing the young men David had sent so that she could have served them. And then she pled with David not to take the life of her household and servants.

Because of her discretion, honesty, humility, peace, and wisdom in keeping David from doing something he would later regret, David rewarded her with these words: "Go up in peace to your house. See, I have heeded your voice and respected your person" (1 Sam. 25:35). When Abigail returned to her home, she was met with the sound of feasting and a drunken husband. Wisely, she waited until he was sober to tell him of the events with David. Immediately his heart died within him, and ten days later he was dead because "the LORD struck Nabal" (v. 38).

David lost no time in recognizing the Lord's vengeance on Nabal and asking Abigail to be his wife. He knew a worthy woman when he saw one, and this woman, who had known a worthless man, now had the opportunity to know a worthy one and took haste in doing so. "She rose, bowed her face to the earth, and said, 'Here is your maidservant, a servant to wash the feet of the servants of my lord'" (1 Sam. 25:41).

What if Abigail had found her significance, worth, and beauty in her husband? She certainly wouldn't have responded the way she did. The reason why she was able to serve the King of kings by serving David was because she feared Him more than she feared her husband. She went into her relationship with David the same way. She could go into the marriage with a servant's heart because she derived her significance from the Lord.

When we try to gain our security and significance from men, we miss the opportunity to know the peace and power of Christ in our lives. He humbled Himself and became worthless so that we could be worthy in God's eyes. In Him alone is where our significance must rest. When our husbands or other men in our lives fail to be the men they should be, we can look to Christ to meet our needs and measure our worth. When we recognize that our worth, significance, and beauty are not defined by a man's love for us, we will realize that we are not "less-than" because of our husband's addiction, adultery, or anger; by His Spirit we have the capacity to respond in a godly way. Christ alone defines our worth, significance, and beauty by His life, death, and resurrection.

Caught in the Act

It is hard to believe the gospel defines our worth when we fall into sexual sin, which is a great temptation when we think our significance and security come from a relationship with a man. During seminary I had the privilege of being an answer to a woman's prayer. She had cried out to the Lord to send someone into her life she could talk to about her battle with eating-dieting-purging since she was thirteen years old. She had been at seminary for a year and was still hiding it from everyone because she was fearful of a condemning response. On top of that, she, a single woman, had never told anyone about an affair she had been in for six months with a married man. She felt far from God and believed He was angry with her for doing these things and was going to punish her. This woman was afraid to share her secrets for fear she would no longer have worth, significance, or beauty in others' eyes. John 8 has an encouraging answer for someone like her.

There was a woman who was caught in the act of adultery. The scribes and Pharisees brought her to the temple where Jesus was teaching and placed her in the midst of everyone, telling them of her sexual promiscuity. They were eager to condemn her in the name of the Law of Moses and even used this woman's situation to test Jesus's commitment to the Law's demand. But Jesus had come to save sinners, and so He had a test of His own for the scribes and Pharisees. He said, "He who is without sin among you, let him throw a stone at her first" (John 8:7). Beginning with the oldest, they walked away one by one. At last Jesus was alone with the woman standing before Him. He was the only one of all the people who could have stoned her. After all, He met His own requirements. He knew no sin. But instead Jesus gave her grace. By asking the question, "Woman, where are those accusers of yours? Has no one condemned you?" (v. 10), He was revealing to her that all have sinned and fallen short of the glory of God. By saying, "Neither do I condemn you" (v. 11), He was revealing to her that He can extend grace because He is the Savior of God's people and has taken their penalty on Himself. By telling her to "go and sin no more" (v. 11), He was instructing her in the proper response to grace.

The same is true for you and me today. Our sexual sin doesn't define us; our Savior does. What we have done with men in order to find our worth, security, and significance is covered by the blood of the Lamb when we repent and turn to Christ in faith. He has endured casting of stones for us so that we might not die, but have everlasting life. And in response to such grace, we should go and sin no more.

Self-Controlled and Pure

But going and sinning no more is difficult to do in a fallen world. In fact, it is impossible apart from Christ. In Paul's letter to Titus, the apostle instructs the pastor in what it means to have a sound church, both theologically and practically, the practical flowing from the theological. Older women were to teach the younger women how "to love their husbands, to love their children, to be discreet, chaste, homemakers, good, obedient to their own husbands, that the word of God may not be blasphemed" (Titus 2:4–5). When we believe the lie that our worth is defined by whether or not a man loves us, we can be tempted to gain the attention of a man, or men, in inappropriate ways, such as dressing immodestly. Instead, we should strive to help our brothers live up to Paul's exhortation to Timothy to treat the younger women as sisters "with all purity" (1 Tim. 5:2). We need to think twice about what we wear and maybe ask a simple question before putting on clothes in the morning: Will these clothes help or hinder my brother toward holiness?

In a culture that teaches us being sexy is tied to our beauty, we should heed Solomon's warning to his son about seductive women: "Do not lust after her beauty in your heart, nor let her allure you with her eyelids" (Prov. 6:25). It is not just clothing; it is our behavior too. Flirtatious glances or casual touches with men who are not our husbands should have no place in our lives. Again, Solomon warns his son about "the evil woman" and "the flattering tongue of a seductress" (v. 24).

Along these same lines are Christ's words to the church in Pergamum. After commending them for their die-hard faithfulness to His name, He judges them for committing sexual immorality (Rev. 2:14). This was a sin that Paul had to deal with in the Corinthian church as well (1 Cor. 5:1; 6:13). In his letter to the Ephesian saints, in the context of speaking about walking in love with fellow members of Christ, he says that sexual immorality is "not even [to] be named among [them]" (Eph. 5:3). How we interact with the men in our life is of paramount importance. Let us strive in every way to help them turn their eyes to the Lord, and if they are married, to the wife of their youth. Our self-control and purity display our belief that our significance and beauty don't come from a relationship with a man, but from Christ. And they are ways that we love God with all our heart and our neighbor as ourselves.

Perhaps you can relate to me believing the lie that my significance and beauty lay in a relationship with a man. I hope this chapter has encouraged you that Christ is the bridegroom who defines His bride's (the church's) significance and gives her security. I close this chapter with a verse I've used often in counseling women through broken hearts:

> "Do not fear, for you will not be ashamed;
> Neither be disgraced, for you will not be put to
>   shame;
> For you will forget the shame of your youth,
> And will not remember the reproach of your
>   widowhood anymore.
> For your Maker is your husband,
> The LORD of hosts is His name;
> And your Redeemer *is* the Holy One of Israel;
> He is called the God of the whole earth.
> For the Lord has called you
> Like a woman forsaken and grieved in spirit,
> Like a youthful wife when you were refused,"
> Says your God.
> "For a mere moment I have forsaken you,
> But with great mercies I will gather you.
> With a little wrath I hid My face from you for a
>   moment;
> But with everlasting kindness I will have mercy
>   on you,"
> Says the LORD, your Redeemer. (Isa. 54:4–8)

THINKING ABOUT THESE THINGS

1. When have you been tempted to believe the lie that your significance and beauty lay in your relationship with a man?

2. How have you struggled with passion and purity?

3. If you are married, spend time praying for your husband to be holy in his speech and conduct, fervent in his love for God and others, steadfast in his faith, and sexually pure. If you are single, spend time praying for the Lord to strengthen you in these areas.

4. What challenged you about the story of Nabal and Abigail?

5. Could you relate more to the woman caught in adultery or to those holding the stones? How was the beauty of the gospel displayed in this story?

6. What challenged you about the exhortation in Titus 2?

Chapter 4

Girl Power

Olivia is a clever, hardworking student who hopes one day to be an engineer, inventor, or scientist. Her dad is an editor for the city newspaper, and her mom is a doctor. She rarely needs help with her homework because she is so smart, and she enjoys living in a beautiful home with a big yard.

Andrea is a performer who loves acting, singing, and dancing. Her dream is to become a superstar, and she is confident she'll be the biggest star in her city. But she is not content to stop at being a superstar in her city; she wants to be part of a world tour. She is so busy dreaming about becoming a star that she has a hard time serving customers at her café job. She already regularly performs in her city—the venue has a sign with her name on it—which fuels her desire to have a bigger stage with a bigger sign one day. She is amazing at what she does and always succeeds in pleasing the crowd.

Emma is an artist and enjoys competing in horse competitions. Her dream is to become the next greatest fashion designer. She helps her friends accessorize their outfits;

they've learned to seek her approval as to what looks best. She enjoys giving them makeovers too.

Mia loves animals and wants to become a vet one day. She has a tender heart and is always trying to help animals find better homes. She enjoys camping, canoeing, horseback riding, and playing the drums. She is very responsible in caring for her horse and is an excellent horseback rider who shows good sportsmanship. She is gifted at training animals; one of her dogs has already won two awards.

Stephanie is a planner and perfectionist who enjoys flying lessons; she is also an excellent baker. She is super organized, never forgetting special occasions and never letting anything go wrong. She drives a stylish car that she is very proud of, and she takes good care of it.

All five of these high achievers are good friends and are known as the most intelligent girls in their town. They are also fashionably dressed, slim, fit, and well manicured. Put together, their appearance and achievements make them stunning.

As I read this story about Lego® Friends[1] that had been given to my daughter, I was struck at the strong and powerful message it was sending young readers. And I was struck at how familiar it all sounded. The message it promoted was perfection, power, position, and prestige. If you dream big and seek to achieve in your specialty, then you will be granted a popular position that carries great prestige with it. In other words, you will be beautiful in the

---

1. Helen Murray, *Friends Forever* (New York: DK Publishing, 2012).

world's eyes not just because you are pretty but also because of your performance. It sounded familiar because I had heard it, though to a different tune from Lego® Friends, when I was younger.

Athletics and Accolades

I had enjoyed playing the piano, swimming, and playing tennis and basketball before my high school years. By the time I completed high school, I had added several other things to my resume. I was a varsity athlete, as well as a member of the National Beta Club, Spanish Honors Society, Key Club, and Interact Club. I had been awarded college scholarship money from Fellowship of Christian Athletes as well as from Eastside Hospital. I had completed full-time internships in the community at the Boys and Girls Club, Kaiser Permanente, and Eastside Hospital. I was a leader in my youth group, participated in mission trips, and was an advanced placement student as well as an honor graduate. I had been accepted to the college of my choice, and everyone encouraged me that I could look forward to a bright future. I was a high achiever.

Without realizing it I was slowly and subtly buying into a lie during those years that I still do battle with today. I'll state it in three different ways to let it slowly sink in because it is likely you battle with it too: (1) My appeal is based on my achievements. (2) My worth is based on the worthiness of my work, and that worthiness is determined by the world. (3) My significance is based on my success as defined by my superiors. In our culture today, beauty is not just defined by appearance; it is also defined by our achievements.

Several years ago I was driving to a conference, and on the passenger's seat I had a few of my published Bible studies. My study on Judges and Ruth lay on top. On the front cover it had an endorsement that read, "Careful scholarship and sound exegesis." That was a kind endorsement, and it is true that I had been very careful and sound in my exegesis. But I also knew that study had an embarrassing error in it. By God's providence, the day I received the studies from my publisher, I opened to a page that had a mistake. In all my cutting and pasting in reworking a section, the phrase "covenant of works" was used in a place that should have said "covenant of redemption." I was sick to my stomach, speechless, and sorry that this error had happened, and I had to call my publisher and tell them. I offered to pay for the mistake, but my publisher was very gracious, and in the end it didn't cost them any money. Even so, as I drove down the highway, all I could hear was the mocking voice of the world, the devil, and my flesh: "Careful scholarship? Sound exegesis? Ha! You don't ever deserve to write again." By God's grace I recognized that I was tempted to believe the lie I had learned in high school. It was as if I was on the basketball court again and needed to be benched because I hadn't played to the level of my coach's expectations. When I told my pastor about my mistake, he kindly reminded me that the covenant of redemption is a covenant of works—the work of the Father, the Son, and the Holy Spirit. Because of the triune God's work on my behalf, I could rest in His grace for that error.

You may not be able to relate to the specifics of my mistake, but perhaps you have blown a deadline for your boss, didn't meet the expectations your leader had for your role, didn't get an A on a paper you poured your heart into, or didn't receive a "good job" from someone you were hoping would notice. Isn't it true that those lies we were most tempted to believe when we were younger are still with us today? To be sure, with the help of the Spirit, we've matured and grown in holiness, but we would be foolish to forget that our flesh is still very weak. I begin each of my morning prayer times with, "By ourselves we are too weak to hold our own even for a moment. And our sworn enemies—the devil, the world, and our own flesh—never stop attacking us. And so, Lord, uphold us and make us strong with the strength of your Holy Spirit, so that we may not go down to defeat in this spiritual struggle, but may firmly resist our enemies until we finally win the complete victory" (Heidelberg Catechism 127). This is a constant reminder to be on guard for the lies that swirl around and within me. We must fight these lies with the truth of God's Word.

Unlikely Heroes

If anyone needed to fight the lie that our significance is based on our success as defined by our superiors, it was a couple of Hebrew midwives who lived in Egypt at the time of Moses's birth. Their story is recorded in Exodus 1.

The Hebrew people had been living in slavery in Egypt for about four hundred years, and a new king arose who feared their large numbers and might. He treated them very harshly and oppressed them greatly. Yet the more they were oppressed, the more they grew in number and the farther in the land they spread. Out of fear and dread that the Hebrews might join Egypt's enemies if war broke out, fight against them, and flee the land, the king decided something must be done. He ordered the Hebrew midwives to kill the sons of the Hebrew women upon birth. Instead of obeying the king, the Hebrew midwives obeyed the King of kings and let the Hebrew boys live. The midwives put their lives in great danger to do so, and eventually the king called them in for questioning. Clever in their answer, they attributed their failure to carry out the king's orders to the Hebrew women giving birth too quickly for them to fulfill the command. The Lord protected the midwives from punishment, and the Hebrew people continued to grow in size and strength. The Lord even gave the midwives families because they had feared Him instead of the Egyptian king (vv. 15–22).

What would have happened if these midwives had feared their superiors instead of God? The entire story of redemption would have been threatened. But instead, these women took the work God had for them very seriously, and they served Him instead of themselves or the king. Instead of believing their significance was based on their success in the eyes of their superior, they believed their significance was based on their success in the eyes of their Savior.

Because of Christ's work, our significance is based on our Savior's success. And our Savior has not only succeeded in every way according to the law of God but He has also satisfied the wrath of God. Were these two women heroes in the eyes of the king? No, they had absolutely failed to fulfill his command. But they were heroes serving the Hero, and that makes all the difference in the world.

A Mother in Israel

Scripture gives an account of another hero serving the Hero in Judges 4–5. During some of the darkest days of Israel's history, the Lord raised up a woman named Deborah to be a judge who would deliver His people, anticipating the greatest and final Judge, Jesus Christ, and His deliverance of His people from the oppression of sin. Along with being a judge, Deborah was a prophetess, wife, mother in Israel, and a helper. She called one man, Barak, into account, urging him to regard the word of the Lord. But Barak wouldn't obey without Deborah at his side. So Deborah arose and went up to Mount Tabor with him. Not only did she go up with him, she also guided him with sound advice, encouraging him at every turn to obey God and put his confidence in Him. Deborah believed that the Lord was fighting the battle before them, and indeed He was. In the light of victory, Deborah and Barak sang a song to the Lord. And Deborah did what every godly leader does; she gave God the glory and praised the people for the parts they played in the victory.

Deborah had the perfect opportunity to glory in her success and achievements. After all,

> village life ceased, it ceased in Israel,
> Until I, Deborah, arose,
> Arose a mother in Israel. (Judg. 5:7)

But this mother in Israel, who was a confident and competent leader, gave all glory to the Lord God because she knew that it was not her success or her spirituality but His strength that won the battle. You and I will be given opportunities in our lives to glory in our success and spirituality, but we must not do that. It is the Lord God who has given us our gifts, and they are gifts of grace. If we boast we must boast in the Lord (Jer. 9:23–24; 1 Cor. 1:31).

Esther's Finest Hour

Along with the Hebrew midwives and Deborah, the book of Esther tells a story in which a woman believed her significance was based on her Savior instead of her success as defined by her superiors. Esther was a beautiful, young Jewish virgin drafted into a beauty pageant for a worthless king who had dismissed his wife in anger when she refused to parade her beauty in front of the people and princes as he had commanded (Est. 1:12; 2:8). The preparation for the beauty pageant took a full twelve months, and that was with seven young women attending to Esther (2:12). If she "was lovely and beautiful" (2:7) before the year of beauty treatments, she must have been stunning at the end of them. And the king thought so too, because he chose her, out of all the women paraded in front of him, to be his wife, the new queen (2:17).

Esther was God's woman for the hour during this time of redemptive history. He was going to move His plans and purposes forward through her. Because of her submission to her uncle she saved the king's life (Est. 2:19–23), and because of her courage, conviction, and kindness, she saved the lives of the Jews when an evil government official convinced the king of a plan to kill all the Jews (3:5–6). She put her own life at risk in order to save her people when she approached the king with her plan (4:11; 5:1–7; 7:3–4; 8:3–6). Even though it was against the law by penalty of death for her to approach the king without his summoning her, she was willing to go for the sake of God's people. She displayed her faith by requesting that the Jews fast on her behalf for three days leading up to her time with the king (4:16). She recognized that favor in the king's eyes could come only from God.

Esther was only able to do what she did because she believed her significance and security came from the Lord instead of her looks or her lord. And the same will be true for you and me. We will be able to accomplish what God has prepared beforehand for us to do only when we realize that our significance and security are rooted in our Savior.

Know Who You Are

All those who are in Christ Jesus are new creations and are beautiful in Christ. We already have perfection, power, position, and prestige. The author of Hebrews says, "But this Man, after He had offered one sacrifice for sins forever, sat down at the right hand of God, from that time waiting till His enemies are made His footstool. For by one offering He has perfected forever those who are being sanctified" (10:12–14). Isn't this a freeing thought? We already have the status "perfect" before our heavenly Father because Christ's perfection has been given to us.

We also have power. Paul was gladly able to boast in his weaknesses because he knew that the power of Christ rested on him (2 Cor. 12:9). Isn't this a wonderful thought? We have been taught to hide our weaknesses and highlight our strengths, but God's Word says to highlight His strength by not hiding our weaknesses. Paul writes, "Therefore I take pleasure in infirmities, in reproaches, in needs, in persecutions, in distresses, for Christ's sake. For when I am weak, then I am strong" (2 Cor. 12:10). I've met with women over the years who were ashamed of their present lives. Girl power hadn't worked for them. Deserted dreams, messy marriages, prodigal children, crashed careers, and fallen finances left them filled with shame. They needed someone to remind them of their identity. Those who are in Christ have His perfection and power. But this is not all.

We also have position. When God saved us, our position changed. We became children of God. Yes, think of it! We are daughters of the King! And as daughters we have immense privileges. We have been blessed "with every spiritual blessing in the heavenly places in Christ" (Eph. 1:3). We were chosen in Christ before the foundation of the world (v. 4). We are accepted in Christ (v. 6). We have redemption through Christ's blood and forgiveness of our sins (v. 7). We have an inheritance in Christ that consists of an eternity with Him in the new heaven and new earth (v. 11), and we are also God's inheritance, the people He has chosen for Himself (v. 14; see also Deut. 32:9). We have been sealed with the Holy Spirit of promise so that our inheritance is guaranteed (vv. 13–14). As daughters of the King, we have the privilege to call him, "Abba, Father" (Rom. 8:15). Our entire status has changed because of His Son.

Finally, we have prestige. We are royalty in Christ. We are daughters of Sarah, princesses, who are part of the people of God (Gen. 17:15–16; 1 Peter 3:6). In the words of Peter, we are "a chosen generation, a royal priesthood, a holy nation, His own special people, that you may proclaim the praises of Him who called you out of darkness into His marvelous light; who once were not a people but are now the people of God, who had not obtained mercy but now have obtained mercy" (1 Peter 2:9–10).

Ensnared by the Fear of Man

One of the reasons we are so tempted to believe our beauty and significance are bound up in our power, position, prestige, and perfection is because we fear man more than we fear God. Proverbs 29:25 says, "The fear of man brings

a snare, but whoever trusts in the LORD shall be safe."
A good image to have in your mind as you think about
this verse is a trap for animals. When we fear man, it is
as if we've been caught in a trap. My dad used to catch
squirrels in a metal trap in our yard. I can still remember
those squirrels in their torment. They acted in the most
panic-stricken way. Isn't that what happens to us when we
are caught in the trap of man's approval? We are panic-
stricken, thinking our perfection and popularity are on the
line. So what do we do when we are tempted to fear man?

From Fear to Faith
David was once again on the run from his enemies, particularly Saul. But his destination was not deliverance;
instead, he found himself in a trap. In his fear he came
up with a plan to escape that involved him acting like a
madman, much like the panic-stricken squirrel. But his
inhuman behavior worked, and he escaped to the cave of
Adullam (1 Sam. 21:10–22:1). On that occasion he penned
the words of Psalm 34, in which he praises God for delivering him from all his fears and beckons others to learn
from him:

> Oh, taste and see that the LORD is good;
> Blessed is the man who trusts in Him!
> Oh, fear the LORD, you His saints!
> There is no want to those who fear Him.
> The young lions lack and suffer hunger;
> But those who seek the LORD shall not lack any
>   good thing. (vv. 8–10)

Notice the progression in these verses. Tasting the Lord's goodness leads to trusting the Lord's government of all our circumstances. Seeking the Lord leads to satisfaction. When we have tasted God's goodness in our lives, we respond with childlike trust and love that cast out the fear of man by which we are so easily ensnared. No longer do we believe our appeal is based on our achievements, but that our acceptance is based on the achievement of Jesus Christ.

The Glory of His Majesty

When we recognize who man is in comparison to who God is, we will be better able to say no to the fear of man and yes to the fear of the Lord. When the Judge of all the earth returns, everything that you and I tend to exalt in our hearts as powerful, prestigious, and popular will be brought low. All the idols men and women worship, whether literal objects or idols of the heart, will be cast away of their own accord as they run to hide in the rocks

> from the terror of the LORD
> And the glory of His majesty,
> When He arises to shake the earth mightily.
> (Isa. 2:21)

Note what Isaiah says in light of His coming judgment and people who have put their confidence in man:

> Sever yourselves from…man,
> Whose breath is in his nostrils;
> For of what account is he? (v. 22)

Ask yourself that question right now in whatever situation you are tempted to fear man—of what account is he or she? When we place man on the throne instead of God, we miss His comfort and kindness. He longs to show us that

> I, even I, am He who comforts you.
> Who are you that you should be afraid
> Of a man who will die,
> And of the son of a man who will be made
>   like grass? (Isa. 51:12)

It is a good question. Have you ever said to your children when they did something sinful, "What were you thinking?" That is what the Lord is getting at here. It is as if He is saying, "Do you know what you have? You have Me, the one who comforts you, and you are going to run after a man who can't even save himself from dying?"

The Lord says through the prophet Jeremiah,

> Cursed is the man who trusts in man
> And makes flesh his strength,
> Whose heart departs from the LORD.
> For he shall be like a shrub in the desert,
> And shall not see when good comes. (Jer. 17:5–6)

When we fear man, we actually give our heart to him instead of to God. And a heart given to man can no longer see the goodness of the Lord. It is blinded to what is good and right and begins to shrivel, just like a shrub shrivels in the drought of the desert. But when we give our hearts to the Lord, trusting and hoping in Him, the fear and anxiety that is a product of fearing man dissipates and we become "like a tree planted by the waters, which spreads out its roots by the river" and bears much fruit (vv. 7–9). What is more appealing to you—a shrub in the desert or a well-watered, fruit-bearing tree? The shrub believes our worth is based on the worthiness of our work, and that worthiness is determined by the world, but the well-watered tree believes our worth is based on the worthiness of Christ's work, and that worthiness has been determined by the Father.

A Servant of Christ

How do we become a well-watered tree? Paul was up against people in the church who were turning away from their calling in Christ and the true gospel to a false gospel. The battle was strong, and he must have been tempted to waver at points and stop fighting. But look at what he writes: "For do I now persuade men, or God? Or do I seek to please men? For if I still pleased men, I would not be a bondservant of Christ" (Gal. 1:10). Christ frees us from the slavery to girl power so that we can be servants filled with His power. Proclaiming the gospel doesn't promise we will be high achievers in the world's eyes, but it does promise the reward of being the servant of Christ. And serving Christ has a far more elevated status than anything this world has to offer us.

When Satan offered Jesus all the kingdoms and glory of this world along with all authority, Jesus replied with Deuteronomy 6:13: "You shall worship the LORD your God, and Him only you shall serve" (Luke 4:8). In the face of the temptation to fear man we must worship and serve

God instead. Paul writes, "Bondservants, obey in all things your masters according to the flesh, not with eyeservice, as men-pleasers, but in sincerity of heart, fearing God. And whatever you do, do it heartily, as to the Lord and not to men, knowing that from the Lord you will receive the reward of the inheritance; for you serve the Lord Christ" (Col. 3:22–24). Because the Lord is our helper, we need not fear what man might do to us (Heb. 13:6). John reminds us, "He who is in you is greater than he who is in the world" (1 John 4:4).

Who would have thought that a Lego® Friends book would spark such a great conversation between my daughter and me about where our true satisfaction and security are found? But I'm grateful it did. The world is teaching our girls about power in a far different way from the Word of God. We need to teach the next generation that our significance is based on our Savior's success. And our Savior has succeeded in both obeying the law of God and satisfying the wrath of God. In Him we have power, position, and prestige of an entirely different kind than this world offers, and it is a far better kind than this world can ever imagine.

THINKING ABOUT THESE THINGS

1. How has your upbringing, present cultural surroundings, or other influences in your life informed your thinking about what it means to be successful?

2. Name some unlikely heroes you know. How have their stories encouraged or edified you?

3. What challenged you the most about the story of Deborah? The story of Esther?

4. What did you learn about who you are in Christ in this chapter?

5. In what ways are you presently tempted to fear man?

6. How can you move from fear to faith in this situation?

7. How does gazing upon God's glory free you from the fear of man?

8. What does it mean to be a servant of Christ?

9. How are you teaching the next generation of women to fear God instead of man and to find their significance in their Savior?

Chapter 5

The Comparison Cage

As you have seen throughout this book, I started comparing myself to others from a young age. As the culture told me what I should look like (appearance) or how I should perform (achievements), my heart began to worship these things. When I looked around and saw others who were prettier than I was or who performed better than I did, I either compared myself to them or coveted what they had, or both. I wish I could say I lost the key to the comparison cage, but instead, I must confess, it is still alive and well in my heart, as the following story indicates.

A Sinful Struggle

I pulled the publisher's new catalog out of my mailbox. As I perused the new releases and saw new women authors and their publications, my heart should have been rejoicing, but I found myself wondering, *Why not me?* I was in a particularly vulnerable season. My publishing career had gotten off to a good start, but my hopes had come to a halt when my publisher said they couldn't move forward with the Bible study series at that time. They wanted to see them succeed and gave me their blessing to find another publisher, but if you've ever tried to secure a new publisher, you know that the process isn't always fast or easy. So I found myself coveting what my sisters had (a new release) and comparing myself to them (Why weren't my studies good enough to continue being published?).

My sinful heart saddened me that day. I didn't realize how much covetousness and comparison were lurking in my heart as I walked to the mailbox, and I was distressed that instead of rejoicing in my sisters' success for the sake of the gospel, I was wishing my name could join theirs on the new release page.

As I repented and reflected on this event, I realized my greatest temptation was in comparing myself to other women who share my gifts and abilities. For example, there are women I know who can wrap circles around my baking and cooking abilities. They can decorate their homes and tables and entertain in a way I didn't even know was possible. But I can't remember envying them for it. I'm quick to appreciate what they do, thank them for it, and cheer them on to win the next cupcake contest. But if you put me alongside other women who are Bible teachers, speakers, and authors, I am tempted to either compare myself to them or covet the opportunities they have—or both. And I'm not the only one.

I was meeting with a fellow author, speaker, and Bible teacher at a conference, and at the end of the conversation I asked her if she ever struggled with this sin. Her reply brought a confession that she had at times envied me. I've often reflected on that conversation. How ironic that I was tempted to envy her, and she was tempted to envy me. It reminds me of the curly-haired girl with brown hair who wants straight blonde hair, and the blonde-headed girl with straight hair who wants brown, curly hair. We never seem to be satisfied with what we've been given or with the opportunities we've had. On another occasion I had the privilege to sit under the teaching of another Bible teacher. Months later she confessed that she had left with a heavy heart that day. She had been focused on trying to make a good impression on me instead of making the Lord alone her focus. How easy it is for us to focus on the positions of this world instead of the position we have already been given in Christ. He has clothed us with His righteousness so that we are beautiful in God's eyes and given us His perfect track record so that we can enjoy a relationship with our heavenly Father.

Your struggle may look different. Perhaps you envy your best friend who just got engaged or pregnant. Or maybe you covet your friend's big, beautiful home. Perhaps you compare your hosting skills to your friend's ability to entertain. Maybe you envy the family next door who seems to have a successful marriage and family life. Perhaps you covet the new position and salary your coworker just received. Maybe you compare yourself to how physically fit and slim another woman in your church is. Or perhaps you are envious of how well the other woman your age is aging, how her children are walking with the Lord, and how many grandchildren she has. Since so many of us struggle with this sin in whatever form it might take, in this chapter I want to share with you what I've learned to battle this temptation, as well as reveal the lie that lurks beneath the surface.

The Comparison Lie
Because of the fall, our hearts no longer love God and our neighbor. Instead, we love ourselves. So our flesh is always looking out for our own best interests. When God saved us we became new creatures with new hearts, but our hearts aren't yet perfect, so we still struggle against the flesh within us. The comparison lie goes something like this: If I had what "she" has then I would be more satisfied, significant, and successful than I am now. This lie breeds a self-centered, isolated, competitive heart that keeps us from encouraging others, engaging with others, and energizing others to do whatever God calls them to do, even if that means they get the husband and children, the job, the ministry, or the contract we wanted.

An Age-Old Problem
The comparison cage is not new. Preserved in Scripture are accounts of godly women who battled the temptation to covet and compare. Let's revisit a few of the stories of women we've already looked at in this book.

Since in her day having children defined women as significant and successful, Sarah's struggle with barrenness would have been intensely difficult and painful. Some of you know just how painful. It is clear from the story that

Sarah was not satisfied with her situation. She finally took matters into her own hands and gave her maidservant, Hagar, to her husband so that she could obtain a child by her. But when Hagar conceived she despised Sarah, and when Sarah recognized it she treated Hagar harshly (Gen. 16:1–6).

This story makes it clear that taking matters into our own hands to achieve our desired outcome doesn't end in satisfaction. The story line continues in Galatians 4:21–31 and shows that something far greater than Sarah could have imagined was going on here. God was bringing the Promised One, Jesus Christ, into the world through Sarah's descendants. The secret of satisfaction is not in securing our own plans in our own ways, but in submitting to God's sovereign plans that He brings about in His ways.

The morning Leah woke up to discover Jacob was angry that her father had tricked him into marrying her must have been a nightmare. Leah had probably heard people compliment Rachel's beauty for a lifetime. We know she struggled with feeling unloved by Jacob because of the names she gave her sons. She thought she could earn the love of her husband by giving him a family. As the story line moves forward, we learn that these two sisters were in a comparison cage. Notice what was in Rachel's heart: "Now when Rachel saw that she bore Jacob no children, Rachel envied her sister, and said to Jacob, 'Give me children, or else I die!'" (Gen. 30:1). Jacob was angry with Rachel's threat, reminding her that it was the Lord, not him, who had withheld children from her womb. So

Rachel gave her husband her maid so that she could have children, and her maid bore Jacob two sons. Rachel reveals her heart again after her maid bears a second son: "With great wrestlings I have wrestled with my sister, and indeed I have prevailed" (v. 8). Not to be outdone, Leah gave Jacob her maid, who bore Jacob more sons.

One day Leah's firstborn son, Reuben, found mandrakes[1] in the field and brought them to his mother. When Rachel saw them, she asked Leah to give her some. From her heart, Leah responded, "Is it a small matter that you have taken away my husband? Would you take away my son's mandrakes also?" (Gen. 30:15). So Rachel let Leah sleep with Jacob for a night in exchange for Reuben's mandrakes. That night Leah conceived another son.

Do you see what is going on here? Each woman had what the other wanted. In one way or another she had believed the lie: if I had what "she" has then I would be more satisfied, significant, and successful than I am now. Leah wanted Rachel's beauty and status in the eyes of Jacob; she wanted Jacob to love her like he loved Rachel, and Rachel wanted Leah's fertility.

---

1. The Hebrew word for *mandrakes* is "love fruits." The Greek goddess of love, beauty, and sex was named "Lady of the Mandrake." The fruit of a mandrake plant resembled a human torso. In this ironic story the woman who buys the mandrakes, Rachel, remains barren, while the one who sold them, Leah, is fertile. Once again, Scripture is clear that the Lord is the one who makes the womb fruitful, not fertility plants. See Bruce Waltke with Cathi J. Fredricks, *Genesis: A Commentary* (Grand Rapids: Zondervan, 2001), 412–13.

The story of Hannah and Peninnah in 1 Samuel 1 shares some similarities with Leah and Rachel's. Both women were married to the same man. But Hannah was barren while Peninnah had borne her husband both sons and daughters. Hannah's husband loved and cared for her greatly. He had a hard time understanding her deep longing for a child. He thought she should consider him better than ten sons! Peninnah tried to make life miserable for Hannah: "And her rival also provoked her severely, to make her miserable, because the LORD had closed her womb" (v. 6). This went on for years. On one occasion when Hannah was in the temple, she was "in bitterness of soul, and prayed to the LORD and wept in anguish" (v. 10). Hannah took her deep desire to the Lord in prayer, and when the Lord blessed her with a son she named Samuel, she committed him to the Lord's service. As those united to Christ, and with the power of His Spirit within us, we can take our deep desires to the Lord, pouring out our hearts to Him and accepting His plan for our lives in full assurance that our heavenly Father always knows and does what is best for His children.

David's Desire

Hannah wasn't the only one of God's people who had a deep desire that had to be submitted to the Lord. In 1 Chronicles 17 David desired in his heart to build a house for the Lord, and Nathan the prophet initially supported his heart's desire. But God intervened and told Nathan to inform David that the house he sincerely wanted to build was not his work to do. Instead, the Lord made a covenant with David in which He promised him a position (as king of Israel, vv. 7–8); a place (Israel would dwell in the land of Canaan, v. 9); peace (Israel would enjoy rest from their enemies, v. 10); and progeny (the Lord would raise up David's offspring and establish his kingdom forever, v. 11). It would be David's son, Solomon, who would build the temple (v. 12). David could have compared himself to his son Solomon and coveted God's appointment for him. But instead, out of gratitude for God's blessings in his own life and in the life of His people (vv. 16–27), his heart turned toward the ways of the Lord. When we recognize God's goodness in our lives and rejoice in His blessings, we are free to do good to others and rejoice in the blessings they receive instead of coveting what they have or comparing ourselves to them.

The first thing David did was to get on board with God's plan. Instead of throwing a pity party, He charged Solomon to build the temple (1 Chron. 22:6). Second, David got behind Solomon (v. 11). Instead of exiting the scene since he wasn't going to be the builder, he engaged with the ministry of building because he wanted Solomon to succeed for God's glory. He wanted God's house to be "exceedingly magnificent, famous and glorious throughout all countries" (v. 5). Third, instead of letting Solomon fend for himself, he took great pains to provide Solomon with what he needed in order to be successful (v. 14). Fourth, instead of trying to start a building program of his own with his own followers, he rallied supporters to come alongside Solomon to help (vv. 17–18). Finally, instead of thinking he was useless, he continued to disciple Solomon by charging him to set his mind and heart to seek the Lord (v. 19).

What if David had believed the lie that if he had the ministry Solomon had been given he would be more satisfied, significant, and successful than he was? He would have missed the opportunity God had given him to encourage, edify, and equip his son for the important task of building the temple. By recognizing God's sovereign and providential hand and by accepting it with gladness, he was able to become a vital part of Solomon's calling. He participated by praying for Solomon and providing for many of his needs. And he glorified God by contributing to the work that would magnify His great name in all the earth.

Christ has given each of us gifts of grace, and we are to use them for His glory and according to His will (Eph. 4:7–8). Paul tells us that we have been "created in Christ Jesus for good works, which God prepared beforehand that we should walk in them" (Eph. 2:10). The platforms God gives us are not for performance-driven ministries; they are for proclaiming the kingdom of God and teaching about our Lord and Savior Jesus Christ, as well as for encouraging, equipping, and edifying the church.

Like David, we may have it in our hearts to do something great for the Lord, but it may not be for us to do. It may be our sister who is called to teach the largest Bible study in the city, speak at the next women's retreat, or write the next blog post or book. It may be our sister who is called to the mission field, or starts the next shelter for abused women, or helps girls escape from a life of sex trafficking. It may be our sister who is given great wealth to support a young unwed mother, pay for the hotel costs of a mother commuting back and forth to the NICU to feed her baby, or give someone in need a vehicle. It may be our sister who is asked to be in charge of the church picnics, plan the menus, help cook for special events, and has the best cupcakes in the church.

Regardless, our response should be like David's. With hearts filled with gratitude for God's great promises and faithfulness to us, envy should give way to encouragement. Instead of secretly hoping she won't succeed, we should pray that she would succeed for the sake of God's great name. Instead of carrying on with our own business, not giving her a second glance, we should take great pains to help her be fruitful and effective for the gospel. Rather than steal any supporters she has, we should rally supporters to come alongside her. And rather than discourage her, we should encourage her to set her mind and heart to seek the Lord.

Without the grace of God and the power of the Holy Spirit, this is impossible to do. Left to ourselves we will always want to have more success than our sister. But with God's power, we are able to turn our hearts to the Lord and His ways so that we can encourage our sister to do the work of the Lord and cheer her on every step of the way.

A Future and a Hope

It wasn't just Hannah and David who had a change of heart because of the hope they had in God's larger promises and purposes; the faithful remnant in Israel did too. Jeremiah was prophesying during the time just before the exile as well as during it. If anyone had reason to look around and compare themselves to others or covet what others had, it was Israel. Both the Northern and Southern Kingdoms (Israel and Judah) had failed miserably, and the great curse of exile had come on them. But in the midst of captivity, Jeremiah gives God's people a word of hope: "For I know the thoughts that I think toward you, says the LORD, thoughts of peace and not of evil, to give you a future and a hope" (Jer. 29:11). This must have been so encouraging to those who were weeping in Babylon. I know this verse was encouraging for me.

A tradition in my high school was the parents of graduating seniors had the opportunity to write a message to their son or daughter next to their name and picture in the yearbook. My parents chose Jeremiah 29:11. It was a great encouragement to me to know that the Lord had a hope-filled future for me and that my parents were excited to see it unfold. But it also helps get us out of the comparison cage. When we believe that the Lord thinks about us intimately and has a future planned for us filled with hope, then we can crawl out of the cage into the freedom that awaits us as His children, fulfilling His plans according to His purposes. No longer do we have to look around us; we can look to Him and fulfill the plans He has for us. But this is very difficult to do. Often we settle for what is rotten.

Rottenness to the Bones
I don't care much for bananas, but if I have one it has to be at just the right stage in the ripening process. I want the peel to be perfectly yellow with no green, and no brown spots. I probably became this picky from opening rotten bananas. If you've ever opened one, you know how strong they smell and how mushy they are. Nobody wants to eat something rotten, and yet that is what we do on a regular basis when we eat the fruit of the flesh called envy: "A sound heart is life to the body, but envy is rottenness to the bones" (Prov. 14:30). When we compare ourselves to others and covet what they have, we exchange life for death and soundness for rottenness. It seems like it would be an easy decision not to do this, but our hearts are swayed so easily toward the comparison cage that we have a hard time saying no. Why is this the case? It goes back to the first lie we looked at in chapter 1—our ways are better than God's ways, and our wisdom is better than His wisdom. The book of James, known as the wisdom book of the New Testament, addresses this matter.

Comparing and Coveting Lead to Confusion
James asks a question and then gives an answer to unlock the cage of comparison:

> Who is wise and understanding among you? Let him show by good conduct that his works are done in

the meekness of wisdom. But if you have bitter envy and self-seeking in your hearts, do not boast and lie against the truth. This wisdom does not descend from above.... For where envy and self-seeking exist, confusion and every evil thing are there. But the wisdom that is from above is first pure, then peaceable, gentle, willing to yield, full of mercy and good fruits, without partiality and without hypocrisy. (James 3:13–17)

Wise conduct that flows from Christ and His Spirit is the way out of the comparison cage. As believers, we are no longer enslaved to the world, the devil, and our own flesh. By God's grace it is possible for us to say yes to purity of heart, to have peace in relationships, and to exercise gentleness. We can find willingness to yield our hopes and dreams for the interests of others and discover power to show forth mercy, good fruits, and pure motives as we help others succeed. Hard? Yes. Impossible? No. As the Holy Spirit cultivates wisdom from above in our hearts, the confusion that comes with comparing and coveting will slowly die and contentment will begin to grow. How does this happen?

Godliness with Contentment Is Great Gain

In 1 Timothy Paul warns Timothy against people teaching a doctrine that is not in accord with godliness. These false teachers were proud and obsessed with arguments that came from envy. Paul told Timothy to have nothing to do with them. Then he said, "Now godliness with contentment is great gain. For we brought nothing into this world, and it is certain we can carry nothing out" (1 Tim. 6:6–7).

This truth was brought home to me when I lived in an assisted living facility during seminary. I had been offered a free room with a small kitchenette in exchange for my work. One of the many privileges I had during my time there was visiting the elderly. The retired medical doctor who lived across from me was a strong believer. In very practical ways he displayed the truth that godliness with contentment is great gain. He had delivered enough babies to know well the truth that we bring nothing into this world, and as he lived out his final days he had also learned he wouldn't be taking anything with him. He spent his days exuding the fruit of the Spirit even in the midst of great suffering. He had learned to be both content and joyful in all circumstances.

Godliness with contentment unlocks the cage of comparing and coveting. Contentment is a fruit of trusting God's provision and plans for our lives and recognizing that the things we are tempted to compare ourselves to or the things we are tempted to covet are not going to last.

Comparing Is Not Wise

Paul has a powerful word for those of us who are tempted to either "class ourselves or compare ourselves with those who commend themselves" (2 Cor. 10:12). We dare not do it because those who measure themselves by their own standards and compare themselves among their friends are not wise. Instead, Paul tells us that we should

> not boast beyond measure, but within the limits of the sphere which God appointed us…not boasting…

in other men's labors, but having hope, that as your
faith is increased, we shall be greatly enlarged by you
in our sphere, to preach the gospel…and not to boast
in another man's sphere of accomplishment.

But "he who glories, let him glory in the LORD."
For not he who commends himself is approved, but
whom the Lord commends. (vv. 13–18).

This passage has many practical applications to deliver
us from the comparison cage. First, we must be wise by
abstaining from comparing ourselves either by our own
standards or among our friends. This is not easy! For many
of us it has become habitual to compare ourselves with
another woman's achievements, beauty, career, diet and
exercise regime, figure, gracefulness, home, children and
their achievements, marriage, relationships, vacations, and
wealth. Paul blows a whistle on such foulness and says,
"Stop! This is not wise."

Second, we should recognize and remain within the
limits of the sphere where God has appointed us to be.
One of the reasons we compare and covet is because we
fail to believe in God's sovereignty and providence. We forget that He has appointed us our lot in life. We don't recall
that He puts us in places of His choosing to use our gifts
of grace. To trust the Lord means to entrust our spheres
of influence to Him. You may be a young mom who feels
confined to your own home after feeling valued in a career.
You may battle the temptation to compare yourself to the
working mom who lives next to you who seems to excel at
having a career and kids. But if you recognize that God has

appointed you for this season to be in your home, making kingdom disciples by His grace, then you will flourish in the field in which He has planted you.

Third, we should be hopeful that when we faithfully serve God in the sphere in which He has placed us, He will make our work fruitful and effective for the gospel. It may be hard for you to remain in a place where you feel unappreciated for your hard work for the kingdom of God, but if you remain faithful to continue sowing the seed of the gospel, you can be sure that in some way God's word will not return void.

Finally, we should not boast in another person's accomplishment or in our own, but only in the Lord. Many years ago a woman told me she was angry that another woman took credit for her ministry idea. While my sister needed to repent of her anger, she was right that the other woman should not have taken credit for her sister's work. We need to give our sisters credit for their work and recognize the Lord is the one working through them.

Likewise, we must not boast in our own accomplishments, recognizing it is God who works through us and has graciously given us gifts to use for His glory. I have struggled with this exhortation with regard to the publishing world. Is it acceptable to post on social media news of teaching and speaking engagements, as well as new publications? I think it is, when our motives are pure and we are doing it to inform those who can benefit from such resources, but I think we need to be careful in our age of social media that we are exalting Christ and not ourselves.

This is what God's Word says. We must boast in the Lord. Do you want approval? Paul says approval comes when we exalt God and give Him the glory.

If we are not careful to take our thoughts captive to Christ, we will covet and compare. I learned that day at my mailbox that I didn't need to bounce my eyes off of just other women's appearances. I also needed to bounce my eyes off their accomplishments, "looking unto Jesus, the author and finisher of our faith, who for the joy that was set before Him endured the cross, despising the shame, and has sat down at the right hand of the throne of God" (Heb. 12:2). Then I needed to thank God for my sisters and their gifts of grace and fervently pray their works would be fruitful and effective for the gospel.

Perhaps you can relate to my heart that afternoon. Maybe you have believed the lie that if you had what your sister had then you would be more satisfied, significant, and successful than you are now. Perhaps you sense a self-centered, isolated, and competitive heart within you that keeps you from encouraging, engaging with, and energizing others to do whatever God calls them to do—even if that means they get the husband and children, the job, the ministry, or the contract you wanted. I hope this chapter has encouraged you to unlock the comparison cage by the

power of Christ and His Spirit, so that you will be a woman
of wisdom who works hard to lift high the name of Jesus.

THINKING ABOUT THESE THINGS

1. Give an example of a time when you were seized
   with comparing or coveting.

2. In what recent situation have you believed the comparison lie?

3. Who do you need to encourage, engage with, and
   energize to do the work God has called her to do?

4. What did you learn from David's story that challenged you to stop comparing and coveting and get
   behind your sister with your full support?

5. How did Jeremiah 29:11 encourage you?

6. How did Proverbs 14:30 convict you?

7. What did you learn about wisdom from James
   3:13–17 and 2 Corinthians 10:12–18? Ask the Lord
   to cultivate a heart of wisdom within you.

8. Spend time in prayer this week asking that God
   will give you godliness with contentment, and pray
   for the person(s) you are most tempted to compare
   yourself to or to covet what they have.

Chapter 6

Addicted to Thinness
and Fitness

I've saved this chapter until now because everything I've written in the previous five chapters plays into this one. The journal entries I have shared with you previously span about the same time frame as those I will share with you in this chapter, but here my focus will be on my addiction to thinness and fitness.

Before getting started, let's quickly review the lies we've learned about in chapters 1 through 5. In chapter 1 we learned about the lie that our ways are better than God's ways, and our wisdom is better than His wisdom. In chapter 2 we considered the lie that we have to look like "her" in order to be beautiful. Our worth, beauty, and significance are defined by whether or not a man loves us is the lie that we looked at in chapter 3. Chapter 4 uncovered the lie that our significance is based on our success as defined by our superiors. And chapter 5 examined the lie that if we had what "she" has, then we would be more satisfied, significant, and successful than we are now. With these lies swirling within my own heart, as well as coming at me from the world and the devil, the context was created for a perfect storm in my life. And storm it did.

At the age of seventeen, I shared the following testimony at the first and only meeting I attended at a church that had advertised a support group for those with addictions:

Hi, I'm Sarah. I'm recovering from an eating disorder. Thank you, S, for sharing about rejection. It helped me to see the root of my problem. It had nothing to do with my family. My family is wonderful. It had to do with a significant figure in my life. My basketball coach was the father figure in my life for nearly eight months of my junior year of high school. Having practice from 7–9:30 at night left no time for me to spend with my own father, so my coach slid into that place.

I was always behind the others. My basketball career had started much later than everyone else's on the team, but I was expected to be just as good and meet his fast pace. Words like "You're the worst person out here at that" still echo through my ears, and all the times he let me know I had let him down. Rejection. It's a feeling described in *Webster's* as refused, set aside, cast out, unacceptable, or useless. It's what I felt when I was around him. I was a useless player who practiced hard but never played. I was set aside as a sub on the side. This planted scars deep within me that had a tremendous effect on my life. His words of wanting to make the best player out of me, how I could get a big scholarship, and how awesome I'd be if I worked out and gained weight. He wanted me to get bigger and better.

The more he yelled at me, the more intolerant I became of him; I had no desire to please him anymore. I went so far in the opposite direction I rebelled against his desires. I refused to gain weight for him and work out. I refused to compromise slimness for thickness. The more determined I became of this, and the more he demanded of me, my whole perception of my body began to change. I no longer saw a person inside of Sarah. I was always trying to please a man I had absolutely no respect for, yet rebelling against his wish of weight gain. I perceived myself as big and useless. I was supposed to be a basketball player at 6'2"; I was supposed to be good. If I sat the bench during the game I told myself I had to equal the amount of exercise the other girls had put in by running. But then I started running before I went to the games, and if I played during the game I'd say I'd be in even better shape than the rest of the team. I wouldn't allow myself to eat after games because I didn't deserve it. If I didn't get chosen to play, I didn't burn off the calories, so I didn't get to eat. On and on the cycle went day after day destroying the body God had given me. It wasn't until the season was over and I could see how much pressure and strain my body had been under that I began my recovery. It was by the grace of God that I have made it through. I can actually speak to my coach knowing I have forgiven him because of God. Thank you for listening. Thank you for sharing. I've been changed.

To be honest, I can't remember why I didn't go back. Perhaps what Ed Welch has said was true about this meeting: "The church can come perilously close to imitating AA's [Alcoholic's Anonymous] casualness in teaching about the Holy One. We too are in danger of using Scripture as a practical 'how to' manual, relying on useful principles

rather than focusing on the crux of the gospel message."[1]
If I needed to do anything, it was to focus on Jesus's life,
death, and resurrection and recognize the same power that
raised Jesus from the dead was available to me in over-
coming my addiction. I had already met with a counselor
whose treatment my parents' medical insurance covered. I
still remember the dark lighting of the room. The counsel
was Christless, and as a woman in crisis I needed Christ.
Instead of turning my focus on Jesus, the counselor put the
focus on me. This is antithetical to the gospel. As Ed Welch
says, "A biblical approach to change focuses on someone
other than ourselves. Change starts, proceeds and ends
with Jesus. We look to Jesus and away from ourselves."[2] So
I couldn't get out of there fast enough. And I had been to
a medical doctor, but while he could check my weight, he
couldn't diagnose my heart. Through it all, the Lord was
slowly revealing to me that I didn't primarily have an eating disorder; I had a worship disorder.

Years of Struggle

By the time I was thirteen years old, food and fitness were
becoming an area of focus in my life. By age fourteen I
was very self-conscious of my weight, comparing myself
to the skinny supermodels I saw on magazine covers and
billboards. Instead of recognizing I was already a normal

---

1. Welch, *Addictions: A Banquet in the Grave*, 142.

2. Welch, *Addictions: A Banquet in the Grave*, 142.

and healthy weight, I strove to become as skinny as the models I was seeing.

During high school, varsity sports became a big part of my life. I spent a lot of time running cross country and playing basketball. I was growing increasingly obsessed with eating no fat in my diet and exercising often. I was beginning to have a set number on the scale that made me delighted, and if I went over it I was distressed. Although I was good at cross country and had an encouraging coach, my performance in basketball, as well as my coach's temper, were very discouraging for me. Each failure was another excuse for me to punish myself by either not eating or engaging in extreme exercise.

Over time, as others commented about my behavior, particularly my family, I recognized I had an eating disorder, but even in learning more about it from educational resources—and being scared about the side effects—I wanted to remain in control of a strict diet and exercise regime. At the same time, I was becoming increasingly interested in health and fitness on a professional level, even interning with nutritionists at a local hospital and medical center, and wanted to believe that instead of having an addiction, I was eating and exercising in a way that everyone else should be.

There were times I believed I had put my eating disorder behind me. Since I wanted to please the Lord in all my ways, and I felt guilty about causing my family so much worry, I wanted to be free from this addiction and tried hard to do the right thing. Recognizing the bitterness I had toward my coach and that being under his control and temper would not help me overcome my eating disorder, I didn't play basketball my senior year in the hope that I could forgive him and heal. But addictions are powerful. And I didn't realize just how devoted my sinful heart was to the gods of thinness and fitness. I didn't realize how much security I was deriving from my behavior. Since I thought I was in control of my actions, I thought I could escape from my addiction at any time, but the truth of the matter was I had become enslaved to it. The very things I thought I was controlling, food and fitness, were really controlling me. I was deceived into thinking I was past my addiction when I was really still embracing it.

My first semester of college was difficult for me. Eating disorders were prevalent among the women I was meeting on campus. I had declared a nutrition and dietetics major, but I knew that I was going to be able to hide behind this, pretending I was healthy when I really was obsessed with food and fitness. For both of these reasons, as well as an increasing desire to go into full-time women's ministry, I called home and told my parents I wanted to transfer to a small Bible college closer to home. Thankfully, they were supportive. There I gave my testimony in chapel one week and learned of several girls who were also struggling with anorexia or bulimia and was able to help them. I too was still struggling:

*Never through with the struggle of trying to meet the cul-
ture's thin and beautiful demands, yet trying to give my
struggles completely over to you.*

During my year at Bible college, I set my eyes toward
seminary after graduation, and due to the counsel I
received in light of this decision, I transferred to a large
state university to complete my undergraduate degree. For
most of my time there I lived in a house full of girls that
were all part of the same Christian campus fellowship.
Living with them confirmed to me that I was not a "normal" eater. Instead, I was obsessed with what I ate and the
amount I ate. One of our leaders found me in the kitchen
carefully measuring out my portions and showed surprise
at my doing so.

During this time I desperately wanted the Lord to
cleanse me from the sin of an addiction to thinness and
fitness and get it out of my life. And yet the very thing I
wanted to be set free from was the very thing I still relied
on to function in life. Controlling my eating and exercise
had become the way I coped with daily stress. Further-
more, eating and exercise are so much a part of everyday
life for everyone, that I didn't know how to disentangle
myself from an obsession with it to some kind of normalcy.
I reached out for help again, this time to a nutritionist on
my college campus.

> Lord, I want to pray especially for Your help as I work with a nutritionist to gain weight. Please Father, keep me focused on You and nourishing the temple You have given to me. More than anything, I want to care for my body properly because You fashioned it with Your own creativity and made me in Your image. Father, please help me to take care of it.

The nutritionist was helpful. She told me how many pounds I needed to gain to be at a healthy weight. She gave me tips for normal eating. She helped me think of nutritious, high-calorie foods that I could implement in my diet. But like the secular counselor I had seen in high school, she didn't point me to Christ. She didn't tell me, "God wants more. He wants us to know him, serve him, fear him, and love him. Somehow, God must be bigger than our own desires—so big that we worship him alone.…Take ten looks to the true God for every one at ourselves."[3] So after a few appointments, I never went back.

> Lord, please help me to focus on my inside qualities rather than my outside qualities. Help me to remember that beauty is not found on the outer layer, but is truly found on the inside. Help me to realize You do not look upon me as man does but You see my heart, and help me to realize that others see my heart also.

3. Welch, *Addictions: A Banquet in the Grave*, 143.

I know that it's possible by your grace to gain the weight and to have a healthy self-image of my body.... Food has been a dominant issue in my life for way too long.... Let me keep my eyes focused on you so as to rise above this, and let me be victorious over this sin that has so easily entangled me. Please keep me accountable and guard my mind from any thoughts of guilt or low self-esteem.

Between the ages of twenty-one and twenty-three, I had the privilege of attending seminary. Although I continued to struggle with body image and weight at the beginning of my time there, this was where I learned to take every thought captive to Christ regarding my addiction to thinness and fitness. What my secular counselor and nutritionist didn't give me, seminary gave me—a full immersion in God's Word, which revealed the lies I had believed and then replaced them with truth in the context of the redeemed community around me. In my college Hebrew class in college when I was translating verses from Jonah, I realized that the Lord could deliver me from my addiction, and indeed in many ways He had begun to deliver me. But seminary was the bigger and lasting moment where true heart change not only occurred but also lasted. I was very grateful to the Lord for delivering me and recognized it as His work of grace. But I also knew that I must be prepared for battle. Any addict knows that temptation lurks around every corner and is waiting to devour her at any moment.

Recognizing that the battle was right beneath the surface was critical for me. I was able to put a firm plan into place to fight going back to an addiction to thinness and fitness. This plan included writing down the lies and countering them with the truth of the gospel; bouncing my eyes off billboards, magazine covers, or even women at the beach or pool; getting rid of my scale so I could no longer weigh myself; accepting key truths from Scripture (see, for example, 1 Sam. 16:7; Pss. 108:12–13; 109:21–24; 139:1–18, 23–24; 145:14–19; 147:10; Prov. 28:13); and being in the midst of God's people, where I wasn't isolated and alone but known and loved. For the most part, I still do these things. I know my flesh is weak. I know I am still prone to believe these five lies we've studied in this book. By the power of the Holy Spirit at work within me that is conforming me more and more to Christ, the degree to which I struggle is different than it was in my teens and early twenties, but I still struggle. Often the lies manifest themselves in different ways from when I was younger, but they still swirl around inside my heart, as well as outside of me in the world. I would be deceived to think I'm not able to fall back into sin or even to an addiction. That is why it is important to continue putting on the full armor of God and praying without ceasing (see Eph. 6:10–20).

Food and Fitness: Friend or Foe?

I can't recall ever meeting a woman who hasn't struggled in some way with food and fitness. For years women have shared with me their struggles with food and fitness, and their battles have included being overweight and dieting to lose weight, using a candy bar for a reward after surviving a long day with the kids, never being disciplined to exercise enough, or becoming obsessed and exercising too much. I have had the privilege over the years to counsel girls (and even a young male wrestler) who were battling an eating disorder. It is important to understand that their struggle isn't a difference in kind from other women; it is a difference of degree. All of us struggle to "present [our] bodies a living sacrifice, holy, acceptable to God, which is [our] reasonable service." And not to be "conformed to this world, but be transformed by the renewing of [our minds], that [we] may prove what is that good and acceptable and perfect will of God" (Rom. 12:1–2).

The problem is not that we are concerned with food and fitness. Scripture commends both to us. Paul says to the Corinthians, "Therefore, whether you eat or drink, or whatever you do, do all to the glory of God" (1 Cor. 10:31), and Paul tells Timothy, "For bodily exercise profits a little, but godliness is profitable for all things, having promise of the life that now is and of that which is to come" (1 Tim. 4:8). The problem is we think these things profit us more than they can ever promise. When we have to eat perfectly in order to be pleased with ourselves, or when we have to exercise every day in order to feel good about our bodies, then we know we are sliding down a slippery slope that often leads to enslavement. As Peter says, "For whatever overcomes a person, to that he is enslaved" (2 Peter 2:19 ESV).

Food and fitness are wonderful blessings the Lord has given us to enjoy, but they make terrible masters.

A Different Response

I didn't respond well to my coach's demeaning attitude and actions toward me. Instead of recognizing that I was not to blame for his anger problem, I bought into the lie that my significance was based on my success as defined by my superior. Instead, I should have recognized that my significance was based on Christ's active obedience (He obeyed the law perfectly on my behalf) and passive obedience (He bore God's wrath in my place). I know I'm not the only woman who has made the wrong conclusions about her worth under the hardships of life.

In the book of Ruth we learn about a woman named Naomi who had endured much suffering. She was living in the dark days of the judges when there was famine in the land of Judah, most likely a curse on God's people for their disobedience. Her husband had uprooted their family, which included two sons, and left Judah to seek food and fulfillment in Moab. Over the course of ten years in Moab, Naomi's sons both married. But tragedy struck, and in the end all three women had lost their husbands.

Naomi began the return journey to Bethlehem with her two daughters-in-law, Ruth and Orpah, but at Naomi's urging Orpah turned back to seek a husband in her own land while Ruth refused and clung to Naomi, committing to follow her people and her God. Both women showed up in Bethlehem at the beginning of barley harvest. When the women of the town saw Naomi, they called her by her name. But note her reply: "Do not call me Naomi [meaning *pleasant*]; call me Mara [meaning *bitter*]; for the Almighty has dealt very bitterly with me. I went out full, and the LORD has brought me home again empty. Why do you call me Naomi, since the LORD has testified against me, and the Almighty has afflicted me?" (Ruth 1:20–21).

The rest of the story is a beautiful picture of salvation. Throughout the book of Ruth, we see that the Lord is raising up a deliverer for these women. His name was Boaz, and the descendants of Boaz would include King David, and the descendants of King David would include Christ. At the end of the story, we see that the Lord makes Naomi full again—her arms are full with a grandson who is in the godly line leading to Jesus. Naomi's bitterness is turned to blessing. Yours and mine can be too.

From Bitterness to Blessing

Often our addictions to food and fitness are rooted in some kind of bitterness toward a certain person or circumstance, so it is appropriate in this chapter to look at passages in Scripture that help renew our minds regarding forgiveness and grace. I had to choose to forgive my basketball coach for saying and doing the things he did to me. Until I did, I continued to take my anger and bitterness out on myself through food and fitness instead of taking it to the Lord and laying it at His feet. By responding to my coach's anger with anger of my own, I was ensnared by one of four things, either all at the same time or at different times: control, comfort, convenience, and character.[4] I was ensnared by control because I felt I had lost control of my life and was desperately trying to gain it again. I was ensnared by comfort because being underneath the pressure of basketball and a coach with a temper were not comfortable for me. I was ensnared by convenience because the circumstances interfered with other goals I had for my life. And I was ensnared by character because I didn't feel approved by my coach. So let's look at what Scripture has to say about these four things.

Control

Our fallen hearts seek what we want when and how we want it. But it doesn't take long in life to recognize that we are not in control of our circumstances or of other people and their actions. If we desire to attain something—whether it is power, position, or prestige—and something gets in our way, it is likely we will respond in anger, frustration, and irritation. For me, the more I felt out of control with regard to my circumstances and coach, the more I wanted to control the situation, but I couldn't. I couldn't make my coach change. And I couldn't change my playing ability, making it match his expectations. But I could control my eating and exercise.

Anger comes when we feel like we are losing control of a relationship or circumstance we desperately want. But behind the anger is a deep-seated fear—the fear of

---

4. Robert D. Jones, *Uprooting Anger* (Phillipsburg, N.J.: P&R, 2005), 144.

disapproval in the eyes of man. I longed for my coach to approve of my ability and my value as a player. When he failed to do these things, I seized control of another area of my life. So what should I have done differently?

I should have dethroned my coach and put Christ alone on the throne. The fear of man will always be a cause for us to fall into all kinds of addictive behaviors, but the fear of God will always be a cause for us to rise to our feet in worship of Him.

When David was fleeing from his son Absalom, whom he loved very much but who had betrayed him, he could have been seized with fear. But instead he claimed the Lord God as a shield about him, his glory, the lifter of his head, the One who answers prayer, his sustainer, and his Savior (Psalm 3).

One of my favorite texts of Scripture comes from Isaiah 43:

> But now, thus says the LORD, who created you....
> "Fear not, for I have redeemed you;
> I have called you by your name;
> You are Mine.
> When you pass through the waters, I will be
>   with you;
> And through the rivers, they shall not overflow you.
> When you walk through the fire, you shall not be
>   burned....
> For I am the LORD your God....
> Since you were precious in My sight,
> You have been honored,
> And I have loved you....

I will say…
Bring…
My daughters from the ends of the earth—
Everyone who is called by My name,
Whom I have created for My glory;
I have formed him, yes, I have made him." (vv. 1–7)

When we understand that this is the character of God, we will gladly place our fear of losing control in His hands and trust Him in our circumstances and relationships.

Comfort

Our anger is often aroused when our comfort is threatened. The pressure of academics, varsity sports, and work made me feel like I was in a pressure cooker. I needed someone to give me permission to sit on a swing and eat an ice cream cone! Actually, what I really needed was to understand the comfort God provides.

In Isaiah 40:1 the Lord's word begins with, "Comfort, yes, comfort My people!" The Lord wanted His people to know His comfort in the midst of exile. It is interesting to study this chapter, then, in light of how God gives His people comfort. First, the promise of Christ's coming to reveal the glory of the Lord is promised. Second, the eternality of God's word is promised. Third, the salvation of the Good Shepherd is promised. Fourth, the wisdom and greatness of God is exalted. And finally, the chapter closes with these words:

Why do you say, O Jacob…
"My way is hidden from the LORD,
And my just claim is passed over by my God?"
Have you not known?…
The everlasting God, the LORD,
The Creator of the ends of the earth,
Neither faints nor is weary.…
He gives power to the weak,
And to those who have no might He increases
    strength.…
Those who wait on the LORD
Shall renew their strength.…
They shall walk and not faint. (vv. 27–31)

What other comfort do I need than that which comes from my Creator, Savior, Shepherd, and Strength? Let us look to Christ! Let us read God's Word, run to our Shepherd, learn from His wisdom and greatness, and rest underneath the shelter of His wings.

Convenience

If I'm in the middle of writing and someone walks into my study to talk with me, I find it very inconvenient. I tend to lose my train of thought, and it is hard for me to get it back again. These small inconveniences happen to us all day long. But sometimes there is a bigger inconvenience. One of our grandparents dies during college final exams, someone has already booked the church for the weekend when we wanted to get married, our employer cuts our job, one of our children gets sick when we are supposed to be at a family reunion, our husband gets a job transfer just as our child was about to start school, or our aging parent is in need of our care during a busy workweek. In each of these cases we want to determine the timing of events. But Scripture makes it clear that the Lord has our times in His hands.

Let's revisit the story of Sarah. For years Sarah had wanted a child, but month after month she faced the painful reality of a fruitless womb. At some point in her life she gave up the dream of ever bearing a child because she was too old. So when the Lord visited her husband and told him she would bear a child in her old age, "Sarah laughed within herself, saying, 'After I have grown old, shall I have pleasure, my lord being old also?'" (Gen. 18:12). The Lord's response to Sarah is also instructive to us as we battle with anger over inconvenience: "Why did Sarah laugh?... Is anything too hard for the LORD? At the appointed time I will return to you, according to the time of life, and Sarah shall have a son" (vv. 13–14).

When our time and God's time don't align, we tend to get angry and anxious and stop trusting that the Lord has our best interest at heart. We are tempted to believe the lie that our ways are better than His ways, and our wisdom is better than His wisdom. But Scripture tells us otherwise. Because "all things work together for good to those who love God, to those who are the called according to His purpose" (Rom. 8:28), we can confidently say with David, "But as for me, I trust in You, O LORD.... My times are in Your hand" (Ps. 31:14–15).

Character

We also tend to get angry when our reputation is on the line or when we desperately want to be valued by someone who doesn't value us. I wanted my coach to recognize I was more than a potentially valuable player. I wanted him to see me as a valuable person. But since he didn't treat me with respect, I grew depressed, which is anger turned inward, and punished myself for not being good enough. I believed the lie that my significance is based on my success as defined by my superior.

Let's revisit the story of Abigail. Abigail was married to a worthless man who did not value her as he should have, nor did he value David as he should have. But Abigail didn't respond with depression or despair because she didn't put her husband in the place of assigning a value to her. She didn't believe the lie that her beauty and significance are defined by whether or not her husband loved her. Instead, she knew her value came from the Lord. This freed her to be able to do the right thing at the right time, and the Lord blessed her tremendously for it.

Seeking our value from other people leads to disappointment and despair. No one consistently attains approval at all times from other people. We must find our value in Christ alone. The Bible tells us that He will take care of our character when others speak evil of us. When David was being wrongfully pursued and his enemies were slandering him, he turned to the Lord for help, believing the Lord had heard every unjust word and had seen every unjust action done against him (Psalm 36). David had learned to trust in the Lord, to feed on His faithfulness, to delight himself in the Lord, to commit his ways to Him, to rest in Him and wait patiently for Him, and to stop fretting. "Cease from anger, and forsake wrath; do not fret—it only causes harm" (Ps. 37:8).

Perhaps you are struggling with an addiction to thinness and fitness or to something else, or maybe you know someone who is. So many people want a quick fix for themselves or a loved one, but it takes time to uproot lies and replace them with truth. Often there is a great deal of shame that comes with an addiction too, and it is hard for women to grasp the gospel truth in the midst of it—we are approved by our heavenly Father, Christ has come to set us free, and the power of the Holy Spirit enables us to say no to the world, the devil, and the flesh and to say yes to our great God.

THINKING ABOUT THESE THINGS

1. Have you ever battled an addiction to thinness or fitness or something else? Briefly describe your experience.

2. Review the lies we've looked at in the previous chapters. How did each one play in to your addiction?

3. What plan(s) did you put into place to battle against your addiction? For example, how will you flee temptation, and who will you ask to keep you accountable?

4. Has food and fitness been your friend or foe? How has this chapter helped you to have a proper perspective?

5. What encouraged you about Naomi's story?

6. What did you learn about anger in this chapter and how it can fuel an addiction?

Chapter 7

The Truth Will Set You Free

When Eve could have despaired because of her sin and her shame, she instead turned to the Lord in faith, believing His promises. She forsook the lie that her ways were better than God's ways, and her wisdom was better than His wisdom and by faith looked to the Seed to come.

When Hannah could have become bitter in her barrenness, she instead turned to the Lord in prayer and praise, believing His salvation. She forsook the lie that she was "less-than" because she was barren and by faith looked to her Savior to come.

When Sarah could have trusted in her beauty or become depressed in her barrenness, she instead did good, did not fear the future, and was submissive to her husband. The writer of Hebrews includes Sarah in the heroes of faith and comments, "By faith Sarah herself also received strength to conceive seed, and she bore a child when she was past the age, because she judged Him faithful who had promised" (Heb. 11:11).

When Leah could have defined her beauty and worth according to Jacob's love for Rachel, she instead praised

God, and the Lord graciously used her to bring forth the line of Judah from which Christ came.

When Abigail could have gotten angry and depressed over her husband's behavior, she instead trusted the Lord and took action to accomplish what was good and right. She forsook the lie that her worth, beauty, and significance were defined by whether or not a man loved her and by faith served the Lord and His anointed king in humility and peace.

When the two Hebrew midwives could have feared man instead of God, they instead took seriously the work God had for them, and they served Him instead of the Egyptian king. Instead of believing their significance was based on their success in the eyes of their superior, they believed their significance was based on their success in the eyes of their Savior.

When Deborah sang her victory song, she had the perfect opportunity to glory in her success, but this confident and competent leader gave all glory to the Lord God because she knew that it was not her success or her spirituality but His strength that won the battle. Her boast was in the Lord.

When Esther could have trusted in her looks or her king, she instead believed her significance and security came from the Lord. By faith she stood before the king and saved her people, the Jews, because she trusted in God's protection, power, and providence.

When David could have compared himself to his son Solomon and coveted God's appointment for him, he instead turned his heart toward the ways of the Lord. He refused to believe the lie that if he had what Solomon had, then he would be more satisfied, significant, and successful than he was. By faith he saw the promises of God from afar and was "assured of them, embraced them and confessed that [he was a stranger and pilgrim] on the earth.... [For he desired] a better, that is, a heavenly country. Therefore God is not ashamed to be called their God, for He has prepared a city for them" (Heb. 11:13, 16).

You Will Be Made Free

Jesus told the Jews who believed in Him, "If you abide in My word, you are My disciples indeed. And you shall know the truth, and the truth shall make you free.... Whoever commits sin is a slave of sin.... If the Son makes you free, you shall be free indeed" (John 8:31–32, 34, 36). Like the Jews, we are slow to understand that we are enslaved to anyone or anything. But Jesus says that we are all enslaved to sin until Christ sets us free. In Christ we are a new creation. And we have been given everything we need to live a life of godliness (2 Peter 1:3). This is a good time for me to ask you, dear reader: By the Holy Spirit's grace, are you a disciple of Christ? Do you follow Him daily, laying down your life, loving Him as Lord and serving Him as Savior? If you are not, I want to invite you today to repent of your sin and to believe in the name of the Lord Jesus Christ alone for salvation so that you can be set free. And please tell a Christian friend or local pastor about what the Holy Spirit has done for you and get plugged into a gospel-centered church. We were not meant to live life in isolation. We need to do life in community with other believers, worshiping God, working for His glory, and witnessing for His great name.

Who Will Deliver Me?

If we are a new creation in Christ and we've been given everything we need to live a life of godliness, why do we still struggle with sin? In Romans 7 we read of Paul's war between his mind and his flesh. He knows God and God's law, and he wants to do what is right in God's eyes, but instead he finds that he practices that which he hates because with his flesh he serves sin. Similarly, in Galatians 5:16–17 Paul exhorts believers to "walk in the Spirit, and you shall not fulfill the lust of the flesh. For the flesh lusts against the Spirit, and the Spirit against the flesh; and these are contrary to one another, so that you do not do the things that you wish." You and I live in the Spirit because we are in Christ, but we also have to walk in the Spirit (v. 25). We must strive for holiness, knowing it is the Holy Spirit who enables us and empowers us to say no to the works of the flesh and yes to the fruit of the Spirit. At our greatest point of exasperation or discouragement we can cry out with Paul, "O wretched man that I am! Who will deliver me from this body of death? I thank God—through Jesus Christ our Lord!" (Rom. 7:24–25).

Be Strong in the Lord

If you've battled an addiction, you know that deliverance is often not immediate. Many times you feel like you are slugging through mud, taking two steps forward and then slipping five steps back. Paul is quick to remind the Ephesians that they are in a battle not with "flesh and blood, but against principalities, against powers, against the rulers of the darkness of this age, against spiritual hosts of wickedness in the heavenly places" (Eph. 6:12). Earlier in his letter, Paul had made it clear that Christ is victorious over all these powers (1:15–23). But he wants to make sure his readers know how strong these foes are and how armed they must be for the fight. He exhorts them to stand firm in the spiritual disciplines of grace, which include knowing gospel truth, believing gospel truth, and praying gospel truth. As we fight against the five different lies we've looked at in this book, we must fight with knowledge, faith, and prayer.

Knowledge

We must fight the lies swirling within and around us with knowledge. It is significant that when Paul tells the church in Rome to present their bodies to God as a living sacrifice, he also tells them not to be conformed to this world, but to be transformed by the renewing of their minds (Rom. 12:1–2). If we are going to be free from this world's definition of beauty and significance, then we must have a transformed heart, and this transformed heart comes only by renewing our minds in God's Word. We have to know God's definition of beauty and significance so that we are not chasing after the fleeting wind of beauty and success, but instead are taking every thought captive to Christ. Paul writes to the church at Corinth, "For though we walk in the flesh, we do not war according to the flesh. For the weapons of our warfare are not carnal but mighty in God for pulling down strongholds, casting down arguments and every high thing that exalts itself against the knowledge of God, bringing every thought into captivity to the obedience of Christ" (2 Cor. 10:3–5). This is why the secular counselor, support group, and nutritionist could not deliver me from my disorder. They treated it solely as an eating disorder, wanting me to learn how to eat in a healthy way and encouraging me to gain weight, all of which are helpful and beneficial. But these were all fleshly fruits of a root problem. I had a worship disorder, and until I took every thought captive to Christ and replaced it with the truth of His word, the strongholds remained. Only the mighty power of God's word could cast down the arguments that had become so pervasive in my heart and mind. This holds true today too. When I'm tempted once again to believe one of these five lies, it is only by taking my thoughts captive to Christ, replacing error with truth, that I find freedom.

Faith

We also must fight the lies swirling within and around us with Spirit-worked faith (Eph. 2:8). The author of Hebrews says that "faith is the substance of things hoped for, the evidence of things not seen" (11:1). Our faith is rooted in truth and history. We believe that Jesus Christ came to this earth in real space-and-time history in order to live a life of perfect obedience for us and die a cursed death in our place. We believe that He rose again from the grave as the firstfruits of our own resurrection to come at His return. And we believe that He is seated at the right hand of God the Father, interceding for us and ruling over His kingdom. We look toward the future in hope that all the promises of God will be consummately fulfilled at His return. And because all the promises of God have already been fulfilled in an inaugural way, we are confident that one day we will be freed from the effects of this fallen world and will spend an eternity in the new heaven and new earth with perfect bodies in the presence of our Lord and Savior Jesus Christ. Such hope fuels us toward holiness now and gives us an eternal perspective with regard to body image.

Prayer

Finally, we must fight the lies swirling within and around us with Spirit-worked prayer (Rom. 8:26). As is evident with the sampling of prayer journal entries I've shared with you throughout this book, prayer was vital for me as I replaced lies with truth. But it is not just an optional tool in our recovery kit. Paul tells us that we must pray at all times, being watchful in the fight against the world, the devil, and the flesh. We are also to pray for one another (Eph. 6:18–19). We cannot fight these lies alone; we must do so together as believers, in dependency on the Holy Spirit.

That the Shame of Your Nakedness
May Not Be Revealed

It is often true that the woman addicted to food and fitness, or anything else for that matter, thinks she has need of nothing, including counsel and community. Yet Scripture tells us differently. We are miserable as slaves to sin, we are blind to the truth, and we are naked in our shame. At the beginning of the book of Revelation, John records Jesus's words to seven different churches, one of which is the church of the Laodiceans, otherwise known as the lukewarm church. His words are instructive for us as we look at the lies we are tempted to believe and in many cases have believed. Jesus says,

> Because you say, "I am rich, have become wealthy, and have need of nothing"—and do not know that you are wretched, miserable, poor, blind, and naked—I counsel you to buy from Me gold refined in the fire, that you may be rich; and white garments, that you may be clothed, that the shame of your nakedness may not be revealed; and anoint your eyes with eye salve, that you may see. As many as I love, I rebuke and chasten. Therefore be zealous and repent. (Rev. 3:17–19)

Jesus gives us the solution to our problem, and the solution is in Him. First, by His Spirit, He gives us His riches that He secured for us by perfect obedience and a cursed death. Second, He gives us our clothing. We are robed in His royalty and righteousness. Third, He gives us new eyes. He removes the lust of our eyes for the things of this world and replaces it with eyes for Him and His glory. Finally, He extends His loving discipline to us. Like a shepherd, He gently moves us back onto the path with His rod and staff when we begin to go astray. Such discipline produces "the peaceable fruit of righteousness to those who have been trained by it" (Heb. 12:11).

He Will Quiet You in His Love
Over the years I've come to realize it is not nearly as hard to teach women to love God as it is to teach them to embrace God's love for them. This is one of the primary reasons we believe that our ways are better than His ways, and our wisdom is better than His wisdom. We are not convinced He loves us. It is also why we look to the mirror or the scale or relationships or the world to define our beauty. We are not convinced He finds us beautiful. It is also why we look to our superiors to define our success. We are not convinced of His approval. It is also why we are tempted to covet and compare ourselves to others, thinking that we would be more satisfied, significant, and successful if we had what "she" had. We are not convinced He has our best interest at heart. That is why I love the message of Zephaniah.

Just before the Southern Kingdom of Judah was about to go into exile at the hand of the Babylonians, the Lord spoke a message of both warning and grace to His people. Judah had turned their backs on the Lord and bowed down to other gods. They had become complacent, not believing the Lord would do good or evil. The Lord was

angry and was bringing judgment on them for refusing to
obey His voice, receive correction, trust in Him, and draw
near to Him. He is a jealous God and wanted more for
His people and from His people. After extending covenant
love to them, He wanted covenant love in return. In His
grace He preserved a remnant. They were meek and humble, they trusted in the Lord, and they were righteous and
truthful—not because of their own strength but because of
His strength, and not because of their love but because of
His love. Zephaniah writes:

> Sing, O daughter of Zion!…
> Be glad and rejoice with all your heart….
> The LORD has taken away your judgments….
> The King of Israel, the LORD, is in your midst;
> You shall see disaster no more….
>
> "Do not fear….
> The LORD your God in your midst,
> The Mighty One, will save;
> He will rejoice over you with gladness,
> He will quiet you with His love,
> He will rejoice over you with singing….
>
> "At that time I will bring you back….
> For I will give you fame and praise
> Among all the peoples of the earth."
>   (Zeph. 3:14–17, 20)

These words are beautiful, aren't they? We don't have
to run after beauty, food, fitness, and other things of this
world when we have true love singing over us. We don't
dare forsake the Lover of our souls for the empty loves

of this world. And we don't need to seek fame and praise among all the peoples of the earth when we already have it as those who are united with Christ. Yet too often we do forsake Him, seeking fame and fortune apart from the One who has been faithful to us.

A Crown of Glory

I have found over the years that women never move past the temptation to believe the lies we've studied in this book, but instead their belief in the lies manifests itself differently at different life stages. For example, when I was younger and had a lot more time to focus on food and fitness, the figures on the magazine seemed much more attainable to me. After I started having children, the temptation seemed to be to compare myself with other mothers. The older women I've talked with say that the temptation for them is similar—looking around at their peers and seeing who has the least wrinkles, the most beautiful skin, the least amount of white or gray hair, or the best figure.

As I was writing this chapter, I received an email promoting skin care products. Their target audience was older women, and one woman shared her wonderful experience with this particular brand of cream that was supposed to produce fewer wrinkles and firmer skin around the eyes. The woman shared some of the compliments she had received since using the product, and every one had to do either with how amazing her skin looked or how young she looked. In our culture today, we have diminished the worth of the elderly and the beauty of age and exalted the beauty of youth. But this is in direct contrast to Scripture.

Job says, "Wisdom is with aged men, and with length of days, understanding" (Job 12:12). The Lord tells Israel, "You shall rise before the gray headed and honor the presence of an old man" (Lev. 19:32). Solomon says, "The silver-haired head is a crown of glory, if it is found in the way of righteousness" (Prov. 16:31). Also, "the splendor of old men is their gray head" (20:29). The Lord tells Israel, "Even to your old age, I am He, and even to gray hairs I will carry you!" (Isa. 46:4). The psalmist says,

> O God, You have taught me from my youth;
> And to this day I declare Your wondrous works.
> Now also when I am old and grayheaded,
> O God, do not forsake me,
> Until I declare Your strength to this generation,
> Your power to everyone who is to come. (71:17–18)

Notice that these verses are not upholding age and gray hair in and of themselves, but the righteousness and mature faith that often accompany them. It is the older woman who has the privilege to tell the next generations of God's power and strength to her over the course of her long lifetime. When I see a godly woman with white or gray hair, I want to run and sit at her feet and listen to her tell me of God's faithfulness throughout the years. As she shares His faithfulness in her life, it encourages me to continue walking in the way of righteousness. How do we do this?

Continue in the Faith

After magnifying Christ's preeminence in all things to the Colossian saints, Paul speaks of Christ's work of reconciliation and its purpose for believers "to present you holy, and blameless, and above reproach in His sight" (Col. 1:22). Then he highlights how this holiness is brought about, "if indeed you continue in the faith, grounded and steadfast, and are not moved away from the hope of the gospel which you heard" (v. 23). In our minute-clinic, self-checkout, drive-through culture, we have lost the appreciation for what it means to be steadfast in something. Do you ever wonder why the diet craze continues to boom? People give one a try, then give up and move on to the next one, then to the next one, and on it goes. But the reason why people aren't losing weight isn't because they don't know what to do; it is because they fail to continue steadfastly doing it. Diets will never fix the problem; steadfast perseverance in the right direction will.

The same is true for you and me as we strive to forsake these lies and put them behind us. By God's grace we have to continue in the faith, grounded and steadfast in the truth of God's Word, and not be moved away from the hope of the gospel—the good news that Jesus both lived for us by obeying the law perfectly on our behalf and died for us by taking God's curse for us on the cross.

All Things Loss

In our celebrity-focused culture, we are tempted to place great worth in what we should count as loss. Take the apostle Paul, for example. Paul had every reason to boast in his accomplishments and have confidence in his background, family, religion, and righteousness, but as a believer he realized,

> What things were gain to me, these I have counted loss for Christ. Yet indeed I also count all things loss for the excellence of the knowledge of Christ Jesus my Lord, for whom I have suffered the loss of all things, and count them as rubbish, that I may gain Christ and be found in Him, not having my own righteousness, which is from the law, but that which is through faith in Christ...that I may know Him and the power of His resurrection, and the fellowship of His sufferings, being conformed to His death, if, by any means, I may attain to the resurrection from the dead. (Phil. 3:7–11)

What freed me from my addiction was not willpower, but God's power at work within me that changed my appetite. No longer did I crave the affections and accolades of this world. Instead, I craved Christ alone to be on the throne of my heart.

I don't do this perfectly, and I won't until glory. Every day I am tempted in one way or another to fall back into one of the five lies we've looked at in this book. Many days I believe the lie that my ways and wisdom for my marriage and family life or ministry are better than God's. I end up forging ahead with attitudes or actions that I think will get the job done instead of stopping to pray and ask the Lord to give me wisdom. There are still times I wonder if my husband is pleased with my appearance. I find myself insecure in situations where there are lots of beautiful women around us, wondering if they are more attractive to him than I am. There are times I feel anxious because I believe the lie that my significance is based on what one of my leaders thinks of me. And there are days when I believe that if I had my friend's circumstances, opportunities, or financial blessings, I would be more satisfied, significant, or successful. But by God's grace, I'm learning to recognize these lies more quickly when they appear in my heart and put them to death more easily than I once did. One of the ways to put these lies to death is to focus on the most glorious wedding still to come.

A Bride Adorned for Her Husband

My favorite part of weddings is when the bride takes her place at the top of the aisle and everyone turns to watch her walk down it to her groom. I find myself looking back and forth between the bride's face and the groom's face, watching their eyes, as they grow closer to the climactic moment when they will be placed side by side to become husband and wife. But these beautiful ceremonies pale in comparison to the wedding to come when the church will meet her bridegroom, Jesus Christ. Christ will then look upon His bride with great love because she is beautiful in His eyes. He bought her with His blood. He loved her with His life. He washed her with His word. He glorified her with His glory. And He cherished her as His church (Eph. 5:22–33). On that day we will know for certain that God's ways are better than our ways, and His wisdom is better than our wisdom; that we are beautiful in His eyes; that our worth, beauty, and significance are defined by Christ and carry the greatest value; that our significance is based on His success; and that we will never be more satisfied, significant, and successful than we are in Christ. "As the bridegroom rejoices over the bride, so shall your God rejoice over you" (Isa. 62:5).

Let us lift our voices, then, in praise of the One who forsook beauty so that we could be beautiful, who gave up His life so that we could be loved, and who suffered greatly so that we could be saved. "For the LORD takes pleasure in His people; He will beautify the humble with salvation" (Ps. 149:4). In return, let us rejoice in our Maker, be joyful in our King, and sing praises to Him (vv. 2–3).

THINKING ABOUT THESE THINGS

1. Which biblical woman's story covered in this book has resonated the most with you?

2. Which one of the five lies have you been most tempted to believe?

3. How did you apply John 8:31–36 to your particular battle? How could you use these verses to help a friend who is struggling with the lies we've covered in this book?

4. How did Romans 7 help you better understand the battle between the flesh and the Spirit?

5. How are you fighting the lies you believe with knowledge, faith, and prayer?

6. How did Jesus's letter to the Laodiceans convict you?

7. How did Zephaniah 3:14–20 comfort you?

8. How do you feel about growing old? How did the Scripture passages in this chapter challenge you to think differently about it?

9. How does the church help us continue in the faith?

10. How have you come to more deeply appreciate the beauty of the church because of Christ's love for her?

Bibliography

Calvin, John. *The Institutes of the Christian Religion*. Edited by John T. McNeill. Translated by Ford Lewis Battles. Philadelphia: Westminster, 1960.

Hatton, Kristen. "Behind the Screens of the Selfie World of Teens." *By Faith: The Online Magazine of the Presbyterian Church in America*. January 31, 2018. http://byfaithonline.com/behind-the-screens-of -the-selfie-world-of-teens/.

Jones, Robert D. *Uprooting Anger: Biblical Help for a Common Problem*. Phillipsburg, N.J.: P&R, 2005.

Waltke, Bruce, with Cathi J. Fredricks. *Genesis: A Commentary*. Grand Rapids: Zondervan, 2001.

Walton, John H., Victor H. Matthews, and Mark W. Chavalas. *The IVP Bible Background Commentary: Old Testament*. Downers Grove, Ill.: IVP Academic, 2000.

Welch, Edward T. *Addictions: A Banquet in the Grave*. Phillipsburg, N.J.: P&R, 2001.